THE ISSUE AT HAND

studies in contemporary
magazine science fiction
by WILLIAM ATHELING, JR.

the
issue at hand

edited

and with an introduction

by

JAMES BLISH

Chicago: 1964

This book
is affectionately dedicated to
the smallest literary fraternity in the world,
the technical critics of science fiction;
and especially, to
      CLAIRE P. BECK
whose name led all the rest.

Library of Congress Catalog Card Number 65-2533

Standard Book Number 911682-09-0

FIRST EDITION, December 1964
FIRST PAPERBOUND PRINTING, July 1967
SECOND CLOTH AND PAPER PRINTING, September 1970

Contents

THE ISSUE AT HAND

Introduction

MOST OF THESE ESSAYS ORIGINALLY appeared in science fiction fan magazines—mimeographed journals with circulations under two hundred. The Atheling project was begun in Redd Boggs' *Skyhook*, and revived some years later for Larry and Noreen Shaw's *Axe*. The book also includes several pieces that were not originally signed by Atheling, but which seem to me to be fitting to Atheling's intent and tone; these came from Richard Bergeron's *Warhoon* and Dick and Pat Lupoff's *Xero*. I am more indebted to these people than I can say for their courtesy and hospitality.

The last two essays were originally speeches. The final one is the talk I delivered in a scared whisper as guest of honor at the 18th World Science Fiction Convention (Pittsburgh, 1960); the other I read even more badly at the 21st Convention (Washington, D. C., 1963).

With few exceptions, these pieces took the form of criticism of magazine science fiction stories as they appeared, and hence have little continuity. For the book, I thought seriously of reorganizing them—perhaps grouping them by the authors discussed, as is common practice when one is making a book out of a collection of reviews. But this didn't turn out to be practicable, for in this instance I was mostly discussing a large number of short stories, and such an arrangement would have left me with some "chapters" not much more than a page long.

In general, therefore, the pieces are presented here in order of publication, though in a few places I have violated this order where I could find a common subject (e.g., the religious science fiction story). The dates are shown, and the reader should bear in mind that statements about conditions in the field in a given text refer to those prevailing at the time stated, not necessarily in 1964. For the rest, I can only hope that a faint thread of consistency to the principles set forth in the first essay will contribute some unity to the group.

The columns were signed "William Atheling, Jr.," a pen-name I adopted for two reasons:

(1) Since I was then, as I sometimes am now, writing science fiction for the commercial magazines in the field, I was afraid that I'd be excessively cautious—a fatal disease for a critic—in any such criticism I wrote under my own name; and,

(2) I wanted to discuss my own work in the column as legitimate occasions arose, and I doubted that I could do so under my own name without my objectivity—if any—being discounted by my readers more or less *ab initio*. (As most of the editors of the commercial magazines can testify, with rather white lips, I have never at any time hesitated to antagonize them under my *own* name, so that consideration didn't arise.)

As on every previous occasion when I've adopted a pen-name, my reasoning turned out to be superficially plausible and completely ill-founded. There is no form of caution, I discovered, so crippling and at the same time so suspect as using a pen-name in the field of criticism. Furthermore, it is in the nature of the masquerade that it cannot be maintained indefinitely, and once it is broken, the critic is lucky if he can survive the mildest constructions which are put upon it. As for the second motive, objectivity is a quality which is put down on the paper for anyone to see; what name is signed to it is irrelevant.

Officers in Missing Persons bureaus will tell you that many of those who disappear want to be found, and—often unconsciously —choose an alias with the same initials as their real names, as a sort of muted cry for help. (Anagrams, because they require conscious effort, are even more obviously made to be broken.) In fiction I have used a dozen pen-names without making any such mistake as far as I know, but "Atheling" was different. It was known to quite a few people that I am deeply interested in the writings of Ezra Pound, and have written about him for the literary quarterlies. Most of these people also knew that I love concert music and have done some composing. Well, "William

8

THE ISSUE AT HAND

Atheling" was the pen-name under which EP wrote all his music
criticism (for a Parisian newspaper, and thus far none of this
work has been translated). Not an easy clue, perhaps, but it may
mean something that I provided any at all.

As it happens, only Larry Shaw and Damon Knight, independently, solved the problem, although there was a lot of speculation
about it. When Redd Boggs suspended *Skyhook,* I gave away the
secret myself. After some years had passed, however, I found
that I was missing Sour Bill; furthermore, nobody had come along
in the meantime to pick up the task of technical criticism of what
the commercial magazines were publishing. Eventually I proposed
to Shaw that I bring Atheling out of retirement for his magazine;
he agreed, and Boggs gave permission.

By this juncture, of course, I could just as well have signed
my own name, but I was fond of Atheling, and apparently so were
others, so I took the traditional course. I have done so with this
book, too, but I have signed my own name below, belatedly but
honestly.

Slight revisions have been made here and there, and I have
added a number of afterthoughts, mostly in the form of footnotes,
or in square brackets. I have been careful, however, not to
change Atheling's mind on any major point, even where I now
disagree with him. He was never ashamed of his biases, and I
have no right to meddle with them.

—JAMES BLISH

*Milford Science Fiction
Writers' Conference
June, 1964*

Some Propositions *Autumn, 1952*

To BE AN AVOWED PRO-PHILE* AMID
fans these days can be a hazardous position, and I'm not sure
that I can qualify for it. After dealing with the newsstand magazines professionally over several decades, one is likely to wind
up as at least a fifty per cent pro-phobe. Dealing with them now,
when most of them claim that they're seeking maturity (and one
that it has attained it), is doubly hard on the patience.

If science fiction is really growing up (a proposition that could
use some defining), however, it is going to need a lot more criticism than it's been getting. The nature of the criticism will be
determined by just how far science fiction readers would like to
see the idiom grow. If, for instance, you're satisfied that it's
come of age already, then it already has the kind of criticism it
deserves: (a) book reviews in general newspapers, usually segre-
gated under a common head as detective novel reviews are, so
as to warn the prospective buyer that none of the books mentioned
in these little concentration camps are to be taken seriously; and,
(b) occasional reviews of magazine stories in the magazines'
letter columns or in fan magazines, usually lists of likes and
dislikes, the rationales for which are seldom stated even in the
rare instances where they exist.

If you'd like to see science fiction move out of the detective-
story kind of specialty classification, and become at least as well
established in the literary mainstream as straight fantasy has
been for at least two centuries, then science fiction criticism

*"Pro-phile" was Redd Boggs' title for the column, though not for long.

11

will necessarily have to be more ambitious. Remember that the
detective story has never lacked for praise from public figures
of all sorts, and admiring that genre has been the particular
hobby of the Grade B, or Christopher Morley type of literary
figure. It's even been remarked that to be able to say "I never
read anything but detective stories" is one of the unfailing signs
of a successful man. Despite all these things in their favor,
detective story reviews are still confined in most papers to the
usual ghetto, and the form never has worked itself to stay into
the category of an art-form. I doubt that it ever will.

Science fiction is at this stage now. It has a ghetto of its own
in most major newspapers; public figures have been photographed
with science fiction magazines before their faces; to be a con-
fessed reader of science fiction still makes one an eccentric,
but no longer a complete outcast. Even the slick magazines now
print science fiction stories at least as willingly as they do
detective or western stories, and three years ago the circle was
completed by the founding of an all-science fiction magazine devoted to importing slick standards into the realm of the aficio-
nadoes. Recently, too, a book publisher was paraphrased as
saying, "Give us a science fiction novel that is written like a
good mystery, preferably hard-boiled and sexy, and we'll print
it and be glad to get it." Is this the millennium?

Or, if we'd like to go farther, how do we go about it?

Before we say that the answer is, "Ask for it," we have to be
sure that we know what we're asking for. This is where criticism comes in. The function of the critic in this field, as it is
in others, is two-fold: First of all, he must ask that editors and
writers be conscious of the minimum standards of competence
which apply in the writing of all fiction; secondly, he must make
reasonably clear to his non-professional readers what those
standards of competence are. Primarily this double job is de-
structive, because its effect is to undermine editors' confidence
in many writers, and to lower the level of tolerance toward sloppy
work among the readers. It has its constructive side, however,
for it's also aimed at wider appreciation, and hence wider publication, for writers who show reasonable craftsmanship.

Technical competence in story-telling is of course not the sole
factor which turns a piece of fiction into a work of art. Freshness of idea, acuity of observation, depth of emotional penetration
are all crucial; and there are other such factors. But technical

competence is the one completely indispensable ingredient; the use of an old idea, for instance, is seldom fatal in itself, but clumsy craftsmanship invariably is.

This, then, ought to be the first thing we ask for. The major science fiction magazines, by laying claim to a "maturity" either already attained or else attainable by a good boarding-house grab, have also laid themselves open to critical examination of the same order of severity as that applied to other mature works of fiction. In this light we'll have to dismiss as irrelevant *Galaxy* editor Horace Gold's recent plea that we ignore what poor stories he prints on the grounds that most of his readers like these stories; criticism and public-opinion polling have nothing to do with each other—the setting-up of a scale of competence in any field is inherently anti-democratic, simply because it always reveals that in ability all men were created unequal, and because the only people capable of setting up such standards are those who already have technical competence, a question which cannot ever be settled by majority vote.

These are the propositions I offer, as a beginning in serious criticism, to the writers and the editors of science fiction:

(1) We know that there is a huge body of available technique in fiction writing, and that the competence of a writer—entirely aside from the degree of his talent—is determined by how much of this body of technique he can use. /Talent is measured in some part by how much he adds to it./

(2) We know (from study, from our own practice, or from both) the essential features of good narrative practice; we expect writers and editors to know no less than we do.

(a) We also know that at least half of the science fiction writers being published today are, from the point of view of technical competence, taking up our time unnecessarily; this being true,

(b) we also know that, from this same point of view, every science fiction editor operating today is flying by the seat of his pants. If this were not so, the authors mentioned in point (a) above would never have been published, but would have been sent back to school instead.

In saying this much—and in saying it repeatedly—the critic is exercising his first function: to "ask that editors and writers be conscious of the minimum standards of competence which apply to the writing of all fiction." This is the easiest of his jobs,

13

since it requires nothing of him but the knowledge that such standards exist (a notion which nevertheless will come as a shock to most professionals in science fiction today). For the few antibiotic-resistant cases who insist that science fiction is too aberrant a medium to be judged by the standards of other kinds of fiction, we can reply flatly and without much desire to be polite that we are not interested in any form of fiction which cuts itself off from human life and human values—and those are the only values which make technical competence meaningful. For this purpose we can apply Theodore Sturgeon's definition of science fiction, which puts the matter in succinct and unbetterable form:

"A science fiction story is a story built around human beings, with a human problem, and a human solution, which would not have happened at all without its scientific content."*

This still leaves the critic with the second task of making "reasonably clear to his non-professional readers what those standards of competence are." It is in this department that the critic's arrogance is tested, since in doing this he is also answering the doubts of professionals as to whether or not he knows what he is talking about. Both these tasks have to be carried out in detail, and for the most part by example—with the examples being taken from current work, for there is absolutely no sense in analyzing the "tension-curve" of "The Fall of the House of Usher" if it is modern science fiction we hope to improve.

One would think, for instance, that no writer should need to be told that a story cannot get along without at least one believable person in it; and that no editor would buy a story that lacked such a person. If you think both these points self-evident, please turn to "Night Talk," signed Charles E. Fritch, in the September, 1952 *Startling Stories* (p. 129). There will probably be a great deal of talk over whether this story was or was not written by Ray Bradbury; certainly if it was not, Mr. Bradbury has a plain case of pastiche on his hands. Internal evidence ("jet-controlled

---

*I quoted this from memory from a talk by Sturgeon; he promptly objected that this was intended to be his definition of a good science fiction story. In the many times since that Sturgeon's Definition has been quoted, this qualification has been consistently ignored except by its author.

sardine-cans") makes it most likely that Fritch is Bradbury,*
but that isn't the point at issue. The basic point is that there is
nobody *in* the story. The man from whose point of view the story
is told has no name; he is referred to only as "the traveller."
Also, he has no appearance; the sole clue we are given to help
us visualize him is that he is wearing boots...and, on the second
page of the piece, "clothing." The illustrator has given him fur
cuffs, collar and hat, but this is a completely creative gesture on
the illustrator's part, and gives the author more aid in reaching
his readers than he has earned.

Toward the end of the story, it is clumsily suggested that the
anonymity of the two main characters (there are no others on
stage) is deliberate: They are supposed to represent two different
kinds of reactions to the second coming of Christ, and thus to be
representative of mankind as a whole. Since both of them are
ciphers, the total effect is to make the second coming of Christ
into an event about as important as the annual Mrs. America
contest.

Certainly there can be no objection to the use of the science
fiction idiom as the vehicle for a parable; profound and moving
effects have been obtained by such means in other idioms; but to
expect the parable by itself to carry the reader with it, without
any observance of such elementary requirements of fiction as
characterization, is to expect the impossible. Both Mr. Fritch
and the author of "The Man" (the Bradbury story Fritch was
imitating) had better spend a little time over Anatole France's
"The Procurator of Judea" before tackling this kind of task again.
Granted that the France story is a historical fantasy, not science
fiction; whatever "The Man" and "Night Talk" are, they are not
science fiction either, regardless of their pseudo-Martian settings.

This may seem to be heavy artillery to bring to bear upon a
story which can be little over a thousand words long, but I can't
see why a story should be excused for being bad because it is
short. Editorially I suppose /Sam Mines, then the editor/ would
plead that yarns of this length are handy for plugging chinks, and
that good ones are extremely rare. This is true, and it is the
main reason why a writer like Bradbury, who has seldom worked
at any other length, can attain an extraordinary popularity among
editors long before the verdict of the readers is in. Good short-

*I was wrong about this.

15

WILLIAM ATHELING, JR.

shorts, however, continue to remain as scarce as ever. Mines is a self-styled middle-of-the-road editor, who has said that he is interested primarily in a good story, rather than in sociological documents, wiring diagrams, or works of art. The bulk of the issue under discussion is taken up by Jack Vance's "Big Planet," a good story by anybody's standards. Vance himself is a fascinating study in the technical development of a free-lance writer. He began with three apparently natural gifts: a free, witty, unmannered style; an almost frighteningly fertile imagination; and a special talent for the visualization of physical color and detail. Any one of these gifts in excess in a young writer can prove fatal, since they can be and often have been used to mask or substitute for the essential construction problems of story-telling. Exactly this happened to Vance in his early work: He tossed off ideas, wisecracks, splashes of color and exotic proper names like a Catherine wheel, while his plotting remained rudimentary or non-existent. His Hillman novel, *The Dying Earth,* is a typical sample, exuberant, chaotic, colorful and shapeless.*

But he is learning fast. In the present novel he has gone back to basics, as he was going to have to do sooner or later. "Big Planet" has the simplest possible construction a long story can have—it is a saga, the primary narrative form of all cultures in the first stages of development. Its sole trace of narrative sophistication is in the circularity of its plot, that is, its return at the crisis to the essential situation with which the story began. But it is still only a beginning, a shade or two of awareness above *Beowulf,* but not advanced as far as is a saga like the *Odyssey,* where the essential starting situation emerges only gradually by implication and the poem proper begins "in the middle." By taking himself back to this primitive a narrative form, Vance has found, entirely temporarily, a story structure suitable to his talents and one which he can control. The result is quite striking and completely satisfying, where earlier long stories of Vance's were not, because for once the technique and the material are wedded to each other. The efflorescence of color, strongly reminiscent of C. L. Moore (I *said* "like a Catherine wheel," didn't

*Vance and several others pointed out that The Dying Earth isn't a novel at all, but a collection, and that I must have been misled by Hillman's calling it a novel. That helped, of course, but all of the pieces in the book share the same unusual setting and most of them have characters in common. The 1962 Lancer paperback edition is also called a novel, which Vance could have prevented had he really felt strongly about it.

16

I?) but lacking her control, this time didn't flood out the story proper because Vance has made structural provision for it. What he will be able to accomplish when he knows as much technique as, say, *Mr.* Kuttner /Miss Moore's brilliant husband, who died in 1958/, offers plenty of material for speculation. I at least predict prodigies.

Incidentally, both the important writers we have been talking about above have been the object of the absurd pen-name detecting bee which has become a mania in the last few years, and both offer interesting evidence that most science fiction readers are still completely uncritical. It should have been immediately evident that the "Brett Sterling" of "Referent" was Bradbury; one would have to have been style-deaf to have missed it, since Bradbury's style is so determinedly mannered that he can be spotted within two paragraphs, and can just as easily be told from his imitators, who usually mistake the mannerisms for the style.* Similarly there was never any justification for believing that Vance was Kuttner. As Damon Knight pointed out at the time, Vance has yet to learn basic elements of narrative technique which have been at Kuttner's fingertips for years; it has been over a decade since Kuttner has been guilty of falling into the story-telling traps strewn all through Vance's early work. That Vance has been heavily influenced by both Kuttners is obvious, but that he is also somebody else entirely is proboscis-plain.

Reprinting helps to confuse the issue; so does the existence of more than thirty science fiction magazines, which makes it possible for a known writer to sell virtually everything he has on hand, no matter how old or how bad. Recently Kuttner has been selling a lot of old material as "C. H. Liddell," in which he may be seen committing the same fumbles that plague Vance; one might be justified in guessing that Vance was Liddell if one didn't know better. The Kuttner novel, "A Million Years to Conquer," reprinted in the September, 1952 *Fantastic Story Magazine,* a twelve-year-old job, certainly also reads like current Vance.

Astounding Science Fiction for August, 1952 contains a gratifyingly skillful piece by Walter M. Miller, Jr., called "Cold Awakening," and a gluily overwritten novelette called "The Face of the Enemy," by Thomas Wilson, which between them manage to

*Oops! See my Bradbury/Fritch bollix a few pages earlier.

WILLIAM ATHELING, JR.

summarize and continue two trends in John W. Campbell, Jr.'s editing which I suspect are going to lead to Schrecklichkeit before long. Both trends seem to have emerged as a direct result of the competitive pressure of *Galaxy,* and both actually are the same trend in different guises. They are:

(1) *Phony realism.* This is a kind of writing which we have all had to suffer through in the detective story field, and now, apparently, science fiction is to go through it also. It consists, in essence, of the minute description of the entirely irrelevant. In detective stories it can most often be found in descriptions of smoking. The character takes out a match folder, tucks the cover back, yanks off a match, scratches it, lights his cigarette, chucks the match into an ash tray...and so on. All this has nothing to do with the story, illuminates no side of anybody's character, fails to advance the plot an inch, tells nothing about the situation; nevertheless the ritual is repeated over and over again. This is only one of several conventions of current, mechanized "private eye" stories which are now leaking over into science fiction, mostly in Campbell's magazine. In one recent story, whose title and author, mercifully, I have forgotten (male character tries to fake examinations leading to qualification for spaceflight—yes, *that* one), the manipulation of cigarettes occupied about twenty per cent of the wordage, to the total exclusion of characterization. Almost the whole "private eye" canon was imported in one dose in Frank M. Robinson's "Untitled Story"; and in the Miller piece —otherwise as smooth and competent a job as anybody could ask —the story problem is again essentially a detective story problem, solved not by human but by mechanical detective methods. I am at least as tired of reading detective stories as I am of writing them, and I doubt that science fiction is going to be benefitted by inflicting upon it the cliches of another and now completely fossilized idiom.

(2) *Deep purple.* The phony realism began to creep into science fiction shortly after the advent of *Galaxy,* under the hands of writers who were unable to provide H. L. Gold with the slick, *Ladies Home Journal* kind of copy which he seems to prefer, and who therefore had to seek substitutes from other fields of successful commercial fiction. (They were extensively encouraged in this by Howard Browne, then the editor of *Amazing Stories* and *Fantastic,* who was a detective story writer himself and who avowedly hated science fiction. Not surprisingly, he

18

loaded both his magazines with literary bastards, including one by-lined Mickey Spillane.) The deep purple patches of fine writing are coming in by the same back door—patches of souped-up adolescent emotion and imperfectly visualized color, to say nothing of the so-genannt irony characteristic of most fan fiction. Young men trying to crack Gold's citadel, and incapable, at least thus far, of distinguishing between the well-written and the arty, are producing most of it. Gold buys very little of it, but Campbell, who unfortunately is almost as style-deaf as his readers, seems to love it. As a result we have had to suffer through the recent *Astounding* writings of Chad Oliver—who probably will write a very good story once he learns to keep his voice down—and this Wilson novelette, which deserves incorporation in any writing manual as an example of what not to do. I call particular attention to Wilson's account of the alien symphony, beginning on page 33. It is probably in imitation of many brief passages in Sturgeon's writing, where Ted attempts—never successfully, but at least with commendable reticence—to describe the effect of music. But this sample is incredibly overblown, depending mainly on a device called synaesthesia which died with Swinburne,* and showing among other things that the author knows nothing about the music we have at home—let alone being capable of describing an alien symphony. He thinks all music is program-music, both in Chicago and on Kelane. I cite this particular passage because it is Deep Purple in practically pure culture, but the whole story is soggy with such overwriting.

One of the tip-offs to the deep purple writer is his dependence upon metaphor, particularly of the "concrete-is-abstract" kind: "Hands outstretched, she was love. She was first love, last love, all love...She was love...She was an elusive quality of race...She was ache and anguish and doubt, fusing now into anger because she was love." Obviously this kind of guff has to be done in metaphor because the alternative trope, simile, demands concrete-to-concrete relationship; one cannot say "She was *like* love" and expect to be taken seriously; one has to say "She was like a dancer" or make some other reference to concrete things. Race, ache, anguish, doubt, love, all these are just counters which can be pushed around in any order without communicating

---

*But it didn't. The antic Alfred Bester erected it into a structural principle in his second science fiction novel, The Stars My Destination. As usual, however, he knew exactly what he was doing, and why.

anything of interest. Suppose, for instance, Mr. Wilson had said
"She was love and anger and doubt, fusing now into anguish because she was ache"—does it make any difference? Mr. Wilson
might go to Shakespeare, who would teach him that the only successful metaphor takes the form abstract-is-concrete—as in
"Patience on a monument, smiling at grief"—the exact opposite
of the way Mr. Wilson is handling the trope. To be sure, Mr.
Wilson's practice has the sanction of writers like Tennyson ("a
sea of peace"), but Tennyson deliberately sought fogginess and
imprecision and nobody loves him for it now. It seems particularly inappropriate to imbed a science fiction story in this kind of
simple syrup.

Not a very good crop, on the whole. There was, of course,
"Gravy Planet," for which thank God—otherwise we should have
fallen asleep entirely.*

---

*This is the noise of an Atheling falling asleep. "Gravy Planet," of course, was the maga-
zine version of the Pohl-Kornbluth novel The Space Merchants, which is still sweeping its way
around the world ten years later. It is easily the best anti/utopia (or dystopia, or comic inferno
—choose your own term) since Brave New World, and doesn't appear to be dating nearly as
rapidly as most members of its class, Huxley's excluded. It ought to be noted, furthermore,
that good anti-utopias have a way of biting back long after progress-worshipers have written
them off--the modern man who goes back to Butler's Erewhon will get a nasty shock.

Some Missing Rebuttals *Winter, 1952-53*

IF IT'S DECENT CRITICISM OF SCIENCE fiction that we're looking for, there is at the moment only one place to find it within our microcosm: In the book reviews of Damon Knight. The book reviews of the professional magazines are seldom better, and usually worse, than the little ghettos reserved for us in the Sunday book sections of daily newspapers. The advantages they possess, in more intimate knowledge of what ideas are old and what automatic gestures are no longer to be tolerated, are usually obliterated by a really towering ignorance of the craft of fiction, plus a crippling desire not to hurt anyone's feelings. Anyone who used these reviews as a guide to science fiction books would wind up owning everything.

Writing, as Redd Boggs reminds us by quote and example, is indeed an art to be acquired through discipline and devotion; and a good many writers—with the encouragement of critics who should know better, but don't—set too much store by courage and too little by craft; this famous judgment on Sherwood Anderson applies to many lesser men, and I think it admits of no argument. Yet no writer or reader would be likely to encounter either of these points in the book reviews printed in current science fiction magazines, except for the scattered contributions which Knight has made over the past few years. Their principal virtue is that they are utterly merciless—a quality which, of course, is not of much use if it is not implemented by the sharpest kind of perception; luckily Knight has both.

If you would like to read precise estimates of van Vogt, of

21

WILLIAM ATHELING, JR.

Hubbard, of Kuttner, almost completely unfogged by the partisanship of *any* author of science fiction which is the disease of other reviewers, Knight is your man. If *Kinsmen of the Dragon* struck you as an incredibly bad novel from any point of view—and if you are a little tired of people who are gentle with Stanley Mullen because he belonged to the fan fraternity—you'll find in Knight the only critic who has spoken up so far who has nailed Mullen to the ground with his own stone-age sentences. If you are interested in the intensively recomplicated story as a technique of fiction—only incidentally because such men as van Vogt, Schmitz, Harness, Blish, and even Knight himself have written science fiction by this method—you'll find in Knight's reviews a more specific account, even down to the asides, of the technique *as a technique* than you are likely to find anywhere else. And if you are looking for a set of standards by which to judge any science fiction story, a set which allows you to look at science fiction as though it were written rather than just excreted, you'll find such a set formulated at the head of one Knight column, and amplified trenchantly in the others.

Memo to a publisher: These reviews deserve collection in a book. /Three years later, the deed was done by the present publisher, as *In Search of Wonder.*/ Memo to any science fiction writer: If you get a review from Knight, no matter how belated, *read it.*

I implied above that criticism, if it is to be of any use at all, must among other things be merciless. It can hardly matter what the author thought or hoped he was doing if the printed story fails to show the objective, or shows it only partially realized. To be kind to a bad piece of writing is not a kindness.

I say this to preface the announcement that I am genuinely pleased by the response my first column seems to have provoked, especially from those people whose work I discussed. I am not pleased because I enjoy flaying other people, or because I enjoy hearing strong men weep. As a matter of fact, such responses rather frighten me. But the fact of the matter is that, in a field which has almost never had serious criticism before, one is going to find a high proportion of writers with virgin toes—and the first man to trample them, however judiciously, must expect cries of anguish out of all proportion to the grievousness of the pain.

22

It seems to me, therefore, that the letters printed elsewhere /in that issue of *Skyhook*/ can be taken primarily as indicating that the topics discussed in the previous column were and are live topics. Such men as Boucher, Bradbury, and Gold are busy people, and would hardly bother to take issue with a column in a fan magazine—let alone to do so in such passionate terms—if they were mildly pleased with what I had to say, or did not care one way or the other.

I am going to reply briefly here, since up to now no policy on replying to letters has been stated, and I would think it unfair to ignore a protest without a prior warning. Hereafter, however, I am not going to devote space in this column to letters; that's not what the column is for, and above all I want to avoid initiating in science fiction that species of inter-critic hassle which has marked some other departments of American criticism—the kind of thing which made Stanley Edgar Hyman compare it to "the mating combats of bull elks." What we are supposed to be discussing here is magazine science fiction, not each other's wounded egos.

/The letters were from Boucher, Bradbury, Vance, and Gold. The first three raised questions of fact which I've already dealt with, so there's no need to repeat them here. Gold's letter was a real fire-breather, to which I replied at some length; but I think it better to omit both letter and reply here, since Horace is not currently in a position to fight back. He didn't, however, fight back at the time./

I took time out this trip to make a detour through the Fall 1952 issue of *Fantastic,* despite a bias against it which I had better confess before I begin to discuss the magazine proper. The bias consisted, very briefly, in the suspicion that no man capable of operating so degraded a magazine as *Amazing Stories* over a long period had the discrimination necessary to run an "adult" magazine. In this confession Mr. Browne may take refuge if he chooses, for I'm sorry to say that the "adult" magazine seems to bear out these suspicions.

"Man in the Dark," by Roy Huggins, is another exhibit in our catalog of private eye yarns masquerading as science fiction stories, except that in this case there is not even any attempt at disguise. The piece is a routine detective story. It's all there: the glamour-profession background which takes the story safely out of the reader's realm of experience; the easy lay that the

WILLIAM ATHELING, JR.

hero just hasn't time to stop for; the bourbon routine; the cigarette routine; and finally, the inevitable pair of remarks which are supposed to snatch the reader's objections right out of his mouth—(a) "I'm not making much sense, am I?" and (b) "It sounded like a bad movie." The responses, of course, are (a) No, and (b) Yes.

Dean Evans' "Beatrice" belongs to the same canon. It is, technically, a sample of the biter-bit plot, in which a despicable leading character goes from success to success until, through a hidden flaw in his efforts and abilities, he brings everything down in ruins around him. This one has the obvious defect that Mr. Fransic, the villain, is not a strong enough character to make the reader want to see him punished for his evils. As *science* fiction it can probably be epitomized in the statement on page 104: "Cyanogen ... is commercial potassium cyanide." (Cyanogen is a poisonous, inflammable gas, C_2N_2; potassium cyanide is a poisonous, non-inflammable, solid salt of hydrocyanic acid, KCN.) The statement which immediately follows that beauty shows that Mr. Evans knows even less about the pharmacology of cyanide than he knows about its chemistry. As fiction of any kind, the story is in a state of utter collapse from the start, because it contains no characters—a fault which is *considerably* less excusable than a few technological bobbles.* Instead, it contains an Unfaithful Wife and a Turning Worm, both so grossly exaggerated as to be comic-strip figures. There is the usual complete lack of explanation for the presence of these two in the same house for three seconds, let alone under contract to each other. The lack is usual because the writer who uses types instead of characters knows that his readers will produce all the proper reactions without his having to exert any effort; they have met the types so often before that they've become quite numb.

The succeeding issue of *Fantastic* is by now sufficiently notorious as the one which carried the Mickey Spillane story "The Veiled Woman," again a routine detective story, with the added touches which have made Spillane the most popular paranoid currently uncommitted, and again a fantasy only by fiat. In the issue under consideration, however, Fritz Leiber's "I'm Looking for 'Jeff'" went all-out to capture the Spillane crown—and as far

*It was my practice throughout to reserve the word "technical" for story-telling devices, while matters of fact were subsumed by "technological."

24

THE ISSUE AT HAND

as I'm concerned is welcome to it. Admittedly Leiber is usually a sensitive and skillful writer and it is difficult to imagine him even breathing the same air Spillane uses; the comparison shocked me as deeply as I suppose it shocks others of Leiber's admirers. Yet it is clearly unavoidable. The hero, Martin Bellows, is Mike Hammer to the life, a man whose sole positive action in the story is the commission of a revolting crime which he can justify only by the argument that his victim *may* himself have committed a crime. The motive—as distinguished from the rationalization —is again the mechanical appearance of the easy lay, couched in a style it is difficult to believe could have come from Leiber's pen. (Can it be, for instance, that the man who wrote "Coming Attraction" with its acid contempt for the current American sweater-cult, is now asking us to breathe heavily over such lines as "He could see her small breasts?")

In short, out of the seven original stories in this issue, no less than three belong to the crime-story category which is already evident in other, more important science fiction outlets; and to the phony realism cult which has become even more pervasive, and much harder to counter because science fiction editors haven't previously been so thoroughly exposed to it as have such experienced Mystery Writers of America as Mr. Boucher, or, for that matter, Mr. Leiber.

Of the remaining stories, none are outstanding. Two attain to the signal distinction of being reasonably competent and crafts-manlike, these being the stories by Theodore Sturgeon and Eric Frank Russell. The Russell is frankly kitchenry-cookery, or what we used to call hackwork before we were inundated by the writings of people who couldn't write their way out of an essay on Why My Daddy Buys Life Insurance. These days we are beginning, belatedly, to realize that even the hack—who at least knows how to corset a story so that it won't faint of chlorosis on page two—may be preferable to the utterly incompetent. In the present case, for instance, Russell's story is at least smooth, deft and mildly witty, which is in such great contrast to most of the rest of the issue as to move the editor into comparing it with Balzac. This is ridiculous; if one must compare Russell's yarn to the work of better-known writers, then the most immediate comparison would have to be Tiffany Thayer's retelling of Rabelais for children. Even that suggestion is possibly a little needlessly exalted.

WILLIAM ATHELING, JR.

The Sturgeon story, certainly the best in the issue, is not quite hackwork. Few Sturgeon stories are, in part because of the author's extraordinary ear for nuances in dialogue, in part because of wonderfully fertile internal details—sometimes just sophisticated sentimentalities, but more often genuine intuitions —which can be found in every Sturgeon story. These are gifts which come before competence, which is the basic acquisition any writer needs, and Sturgeon has many other gifts which hardly need to be mentioned at this late date.

The two gifts which I have mentioned in the previous paragraph were also evident a long time ago, and I mentioned them only because they are the only two which are visible in the present story. I wonder, for instance, what has happened to Sturgeon's gift of invention. Every story he has contributed to the field over the past two years has dealt in one way or another with syzygy, which, to be sure, is a fascinating biological arrangement with a (limited) number of symbolic overtones for a fiction writer, but which Sturgeon himself handled definitively in a yarn called "The Perfect Host" which appeared long ago in *Weird Tales* (November, 1948). Evidently the subject has a special significance for him, for he has been worrying it ever since, and not, it seems to me, to nearly as good a purpose.

Nevertheless, "The Sex Opposite" is worth reading for itself, and takes on added stature by being in such bad company.

In contrast, the December, 1952 issue of *The Magazine of Fantasy and Science Fiction*—a magazine as pretentious as *Fantastic*, but more quietly and certainly so, and with better reason —is remarkably good even by the toughest standards which I think fair to apply at this juncture. This is the usual level of performance of these two editors who, like Browne, are operating in the face of one of my strongest prejudices, but who manage to overcome it with great regularity. The bias of mine which is operating here is the conviction that straight fantasy needs no special outlets at this very late date, and that those who maintain that there is no real, essential difference between science fiction and fantasy—and their respective audiences—probably are encouraging bad stories in both sub-idioms.

I doubt, however, that Anthony Boucher and J. Francis McComas could operate as well as they do without their highly selective receptiveness to straight fantasy, and their instinctive rejection of the purely technological science fiction story. These biases on their part do tend to eliminate one of the most exciting kinds of science fiction, the story in which the writer exploits special technological knowledge to create a situation of continuous surprise and excitement, not through tricks of plotting such as those van Vogt usually grinds through, but instead through intensive study of what a given idea might mean in terms of other ideas.

"The Poisoner," Charles Harness' story in this issue, seems to me to represent about the ultimate in what these two editors are willing to accept from a writer who works with ideas primarily. It is not nearly as good for Harness as was "Time Trap" or a number of other Harness pieces which other magazines found themselves able to accept. Harness' style is generally stodgy, and his handling of conversation is particularly leaden. His primary gift is invention; every thought that he has seems to lead to at least six others. He is, in addition, one of the best— and I think *the* best—exponents of the extensively recomplicated plot. Unlike van Vogt's, Harness' packed plots contain no loose ends and work out to rounded wholes which the reader and the student writer can study with confidence. In addition, Harness often invokes fragments of our cultural heritage to justify quiet and telling imitations of past masters in the mainstream of literature: For instance, his invocation of the Ballad of the Sword in Rostand's "Cyrano," through a striking parallel between fencing and formal logic (v. Harness' novel, *Flight into Yesterday*, Bouregy and Curl, 1953).

But Harness cannot use his skills at their best in a short story. They require exposition. Thus far, Boucher and McComas have not given Harness the length in which he works best, nor have they, in more general terms, devoted more than an insignificant fraction of their space to science fiction of this kind. At present I am inclined to guess that this deficiency springs from an inherent distaste for the genus, but I have been wrong on just the point before: It was once my feeling that Horace Gold did not even realize that this kind of science fiction existed, or else that he felt that it was too identified with Campbell for him to touch it. As matters turned out, Gold was well aware that the genus existed, and wanted to print it—but he wanted to print it in *novel length*, and did, as soon as two such novels were offered to him.

Thus the recent announcement that *The Magazine of Fantasy and Science Fiction* will be printing longer stories in the future may mean that the prodigally-inventive kind of science fiction may get better representation. I hope so, for it is one of the most characteristic kinds of science fiction, and is almost alone among the various methods which is exclusive to our field; and several of the very best writers in that field, including Harness himself, write nothing else.

Those of you who have already come to hate me fondly should gather round at this point, for I'm about to rush in where angels fear to tread. I propose now to level the critical pen at C. M. Kornbluth. As almost everybody knows by now, Cyril has been one of the best writers in the business for a long time, and "The Goodly Creatures" shows some of the reasons why. As a study in construction alone a book could be written about it. Even the obvious rhetorical devices in it are extraordinarily subtle for our field: The careful circularity of the story, flagged with the correspondence between first and last lines; the switching of the names of the off-stage villain and the on-stage hero; the motto, "...really creative synthesis of Pinero and Shaw..." which runs through the yarn like a Wagnerian leitmotif for Guilt; the perfectly balanced interplay of many personalities split up among only a few characters; and so on. This is the work of a virtuoso.

And those who complain, of such writers as Ray Bradbury, that much recent science fiction isn't sufficiently realistic should have found their champion in Kornbluth. When he sets out to give you a public relations firm, its structure, its operations, the kinds of men who gravitate toward such forms of organized lying, he does so. He does something more: He epitomizes it. Greenhough and Brady is all PR companies rolled into one jittering package. /For whatever the parlor analysts care to make of it, I was working for a PR firm when I wrote this paragraph—and I still do./

But is "The Goodly Creatures" science fiction? I depose that it is not. One need perform only one simple operation on the story to establish this: Simply move the date back to the present. This move, perforce, transforms Libonari's spaceman's union into something like the Brotherhood of Railway Trainmen, and the Kumfyseets account into that of an outfit supplying Pullman cushions. Would the story be changed?

Nope. "The Goodly Creatures," plainly, is a human story, with a human problem, and a human solution, and told with flawless taste and skill to boot—but it could happen very easily without its scientific content. As a matter of fact, it happens almost daily along Madison Avenue and other seats of American culture.

In short, what Messrs. Kornbluth, Boucher, and McComas have here is a space opera—a highly sophisticated one, but space opera all the same. I for one wish Kornbluth *had* set it in the present, and sold it for two million dollars and a ham sandwich to a top slick. It's a fine job and deserves to be read for what it is, a brilliantly acid piece of social satire, with no science fiction content whatsoever.

This particular yarn epitomizes *F&SF*. It is wonderfully written, but it is also something of a sell. Most of Boucher's and McComas' magazine thus far could be described without undue harshness in the same terms. Because these two editors like fantasy (not just raw weird tales), they begin with a taste for decent writing shared by few other editors in the field. Fantasy is, after all, several thousand years old in its mature, fully developed form, which can hardly be said of science fiction. Asking that science fiction stories be as well written and as sophisticated as most good fantasies is bound to mean that the overall score of *F&SF* in these categories is going to be high—higher, say than that of a magazine edited by someone who burns to print nothing but the best, but doesn't know it when he sees it, or mistakes some palpable amateur for a genius. But in this case it has also meant that good writing and a reasonable degree of sophistication may be *all* a story needs to pass Boucher and McComas. This results in disappointments in a specialized audience which, among other things, has shown itself willing to put up with a good deal of crudity in technique for the sake of freshness of ideas.

In the December, 1952 *Astounding,* the conclusion of "The Currents of Space" leaves us with another reasonable but dull Asimov novel on our hands. If the comments of my immediate acquaintances don't mislead me, all of Isaac's recent work has left many readers feeling, "Yes, it's good all right—but somehow it doesn't hit me." Or (almost as frequent a comment): "It let down at the end." What, specifically, is the matter? Certainly these yarns don't in actuality let down at the end; as a matter of fact, "The Currents of Space" ends with a series of beautifully planted surprises and a neat touch of pure sentiment to cap them. This is what we should expect to get from Isaac, and it is just what he gives us. Why do we feel let down?

WILLIAM ATHELING, JR.

The main reason, I believe, is stylistic. Asimov is a highly circumstantial writer, sharing with Heinlein and with Norman L. Knight the ability to visualize his imagined world in great detail, so that it seems lived-in and perfectly believable. He does not, however, share Heinlein's lightness of touch; instead, he more closely resembles the elder Knight (no relation to Damon Knight) in writing everything with considerable weight and solidity, turning each sentence into a proposition, a sort of lawyer's prose which is clear without at any time becoming pellucid.

This kind of style is perfectly suited to a story which is primarily reflective in character, such as Asimov's recent robot yarns. It is also just what is required for a story in which history is the hero and the fate of empires is under debate. What Asimov has been writing lately, however, beginning with "The Stars, Like Dust," has been the action story, to which he seems to have turned more or less at random after his long "Foundation" project reached its culmination. And the action story simply cannot be written in that kind of style. Why? Because a style that ponderous, that portentous, constantly promises to the reader much more than even the most complex action story can deliver. The tone of "The Currents of Space" justified any reader in expecting that in the last installment Asimov would at the very least rend the heavens in twain. The plot provided no such encouragement, but the style did. Instead, Asimov blew up one sun under circumstances that could hurt nobody but one man who wanted to die, and we are left wondering why this very workmanlike novel "somehow" didn't satisfy us, why it "let down at the end."

The lead novelette in this issue of *Astounding* offers us another example of the phenomenal speed with which Raymond F. Jones can beat his fellow writers to the tape with a story based upon a Campbell editorial. In this instance the result is by no means to be despised. Like almost all Jones stories, its center of being is theoretical, but unlike many of them, it makes a special study of the personalities which might become involved in its kind of problem and thus comes off rather well. The concept itself is fascinating, and precisely the kind of idea I would like to see Boucher and McComas, or Gold for that matter, recognize as a genuine source of excitement for many—if not most—science fiction enthusiasts. There is really no good reason why this kind of story must continue to appear almost solely in *Astounding*. If other editors were to encourage it, they would almost certainly

30

get work of this kind from better writers than Jones, who—perhaps because he is in too much of a hurry to get there first—rarely writes as meaty and satisfying a story of ideas as "Noise Level."

This issue also offers a nice question: Why does it now take two writers to do badly what one writer did well years ago? Why, specifically, do two men who seem to know something about the craft of fiction, Mack Reynolds and Fredric Brown, waste their time on "Me and Flapjack and the Martians," a coy and heavy-footed imitation of "Homo Saps"—and why does Campbell waste his money printing it, especially since his magazine was responsible for the appearance of "Homo Saps" (a 1941 story by Eric Frank Russell) in the first place? As for "Pest," the story by Randall Garrett and Lou Tabakow, with its cuddly animals with the telepathic ears, nausea is not enough. I can only suggest that both authors—not their story, but the authors themselves—be piled in the middle of the floor and set fire to.* The man who should apply the match is Stanley G. Weinbaum.

---

*Alas that it wasn't done. Mr. Tabakow has committed few crimes since, but Mr. Garrett went on to become the most indefatigable co-author of second-hand stories in the history of science fiction, with such latter-day Tabakows as Robert Silverberg and Larry M. Harris. Simultaneously, he succeeded Jones as an instant mirror of Mr. Campbell's ideas, because unlike Jones no firm ideas of his own ever impeded the process.

I would take some pride in having called this three-cushion shot so early, were it not for the fact that there is imbedded in Mr. Garrett's several million words of trash one superb story ("The Hunting Lodge") and enough additional scattered fragments to suggest that it wasn't lack of talent that dictated his subsequent career. While I don't mean to absolve him, I can only wonder what might have happened had he fallen into the hands of an editor who might have fostered his gifts instead of overwhelming them. Even now it may not be too late to try it.

Rebuttals, Token Punches, and Violence
Spring, 1953

Sᴉɴᴄᴇ ᴛʜɪs ᴄᴏʟᴜᴍɴ ʙᴇɢᴀɴ, ᴀ ɴᴜᴍ-ber of people have taken issue with the Sturgeon formulation that I appropriated as defining science fiction. The general tenor of the comments has been that the formulation is too loose to be useful—several of its critics, for instance, have made L. Sprague de Camp's point that as a definition it admits *Arrowsmith*—and a number of improvements have been suggested. Damon Knight wrote: "All Sturgeon's definition needs is the word 'speculative' in front of the word 'science,' for people who insist that 'science' has to be included; for others, the word 'speculative' *instead of* the word 'science.'" (Italicising mine.)

There are a number of questions which could be raised here if they were not all off the subject, among which the most interesting might be: What constitutes speculation? Actually, however, it seems to me that the trouble lies in my having called the Sturgeon formulation a "definition" in the first place. (Ted himself calls it a Rule.) The virtue which inheres in it is not that it defines or fails to define what a science fiction story is, so that he who runs may read. What it does do is to make unmistakable what is needed for a good science fiction story. (And if it includes *Arrowsmith*, so much the better; had that novel been printed at the same time that Wells' early novels appeared, nobody would have questioned its status as science fiction. It seems to me that it is still science fiction, regardless of whether or not it includes some of the more conventional gestures of the idiom.)*

Indeed, I can think of no function for a definition of science fiction which would be of interest to anyone but a librarian, except the function of telling us how to measure critically a specimen at hand. To say that a story *is* a science fiction story is about as useful as to say that a play is a comedy. The whole discussion is a matter of taxonomy. What we want is a measure of worth. Damon's addition might or might not help the librarian —though I think that his original ruling, that science fiction is what we mean when we point to it, would probably be more useful in the end—but it is not of much use in value judgments. It would be better, I think, to remember the word "good" in the Sturgeon definition, and then abandon the question of classification as essentially sterile. ⟨Such definitions of science fiction and fantasy as I am currently prepared to offer may be found in the articles on those subjects in the latest Grolier Encyclopedia. They will be a big disappointment to those who find safety only in pigeon-holes.⟩

There have also been a few letters and comments which have espoused the position that objective standards for writing cannot be formulated, and that for this reason Atheling's strictures can be enjoyed or discounted solely as expressions of his own personal taste. Most of the letter-writers who made this point were authors whom I had taken to task, but disinterested observers like Jack Speer also brought it up. Sorry, gentlemen, but this refuge is only about as good a hidey-hole as the one to which the ostrich legendarily retreats, as I can show very easily from your own practice. You would agree with me, I think, that one of the basic assumptions of our common practice is that the deus ex machina is no longer a tolerable plot device: To have the villain of a story struck down by lightning at the crucial moment, thus allowing the plot-problem to be solved arbitrarily, and through no effort on the part of the leading character, is bad plotting. This is not a point which comes from Bill Atheling's exclusive and personal taste; it is part of the body of technique with which all fiction writers work.

Another example: No skilled writer known to me would defend

---

*But there is now a whole sub-group of novels like it, with distinct diagnostic signs of its own, which we might call "novels about science" or "fiction about science." Maybe Damon's addition has become necessary after all.

the practice—very common among beginners—of substituting funny hats for characterization. To say that a given character always wears a helicopter beanie, or always spits on his hands before speaking, or always takes two steps to the north and one to the west before washing his face, is to put a tag on him which will enable the reader to place him whenever he appears, but it is not *all* that a writer must do to characterize that character; many incompetent writers, all the same, never go farther with characterization than this kind of tagging.

What Speer apparently wants, as do most of my other correspondents on this subject, is a list of the objective technical standards which I will apply to magazine fiction (such as the two cited just above). I will be glad to oblige them if they will have patience. To expose such standards at length would take a long book, for which Redd Boggs lacks space. I will; however, bring these points up seriatim in the course of my reviews, as indeed I've been doing from the beginning. If Speer and the rest will look back at the first column, for instance, they will find the following points made, during discussion of specific stories:

(1) Story characters need names and physical descriptions.*

(2) Stories rich in detail demand special attention to balanced plot construction.

(3) The minute description of the entirely irrelevant does not constitute realism.

(4) Metaphors which take the form "concrete-is-abstract" are imprecise, untenable, and characteristic of over-writing.

There are more in the first column for the reader who reads. The second column contains an even larger quota of such objective criteria for writing. I am not going to list them here again because, to put the matter bluntly, it is my job to write the column —not to read it for you as well. If you gentlemen would like to argue with me further, please try at least to listen before you raise your hands.

One of the natural consequences of the fact that the market can now absorb everything a ten per cent competent writer can turn out is the enormous number of one-punch stories the orey-eyed reader finds in his magazines. For those to whom the term

*True in general, but too sweeping. It's a waste of effort to describe, and downright confusing to name, people who are to appear only once, and most other walk-ons and spearcarriers (servants, policemen, messengers, etc.).

WILLIAM ATHELING, JR.

"one-punch" isn't self-explanatory, I offer an admirable evocation of the breed from a recent article by Frank O'Connor: "...the sort of yarn, so popular with magazine editors, which ends, usually in italics, *'The face was the face of Minkie, the cat, but the whiskers were the whiskers of Colonel Claude Combpyne.'"*

Most new writers and a few old pros apparently believe that no other kind of short story exists—that, in short, it is impossible to write a short story with more than one idea in it, or one without a surprise ending. Out of seven issues of science fiction magazines before me for the January-March quarter, the following stories are one-punchers: "The Captives" (Julian Chain), "Secret" (Lee Cahn), "Stamp from Moscow" (Steve Benedict), "Fool's Mate" (Robert Sheckley), "The Mask of Demeter" (Pearson and Corwin),* "Joy Ride" (William Campbell Gault), "Earthman's Choice" (Roger Dee), "The Defenders" (Philip K. Dick), "Teething Ring" (James Causey), "Prott" (Margaret St. Clair), "Watchbird" (Robert Sheckley), "Know Thy Neighbor" (Elisabeth R. Lewis), and "Secret of the House" (H. H. Holmes).

It is an instructive list, not alone because of its length, but also because it represents the selections of the five best editors in the field (Campbell, Gold, del Rey, Boucher, McComas) and includes more than a few familiar authors (including Mr. Boucher himself, as "H. H. Holmes"). It is instructive also because it affords excellent illustrations of the various accidents which may happen to the one-punch story in science fiction.

The punch, for instance, may be given away by the illustration, as it was in "Stamp from Moscow"; once you had seen the stamp, you knew the entire story (which contained neither characters nor incidents, anyhow).

Secondly, the reader—and in particular the science fiction reader—may see the punch pages ahead of the point at which the author wants to deliver it, leaving the author (to shift the metaphor) with no trump to play. This is what happens in fully half of these stories to my eye; depending upon your experience and the amount of fun you get out of out-guessing a writer, your score may be either lower or higher than mine, but you are certain to have had the experience at least once in any list of one-punchers this long.

---

*The belated appearance of this antique collaboration so upset C. M. Kornbluth, whose pseudonym "Cecil Corwin" was, that he wrote a story explaining that the hapless Corwin had been confined in a mental hospital under LSD-25 since around 1950. The story also contains an attack on the agent who sold the collaboration without Kornbluth's permission.

THE ISSUE AT HAND

Third, the author himself may telegraph the punch. In "Watch-bird," the reader, having watched the leading character pull the standard science fiction stupidity of failing to attach a Control to a Supposedly Benevolent Machine, is hardly going to be surprised when exactly the same stupidity is committed again. What with all the muttering that goes on in the story about there-being-something-w r o n g-but-I-just-can't-put-my-f i n g e r-on-it,* the reader may have seen ahead of Sheckley the *first* time it happened.

A kind of sub-class of this sort of telegraphing is represented in the list by the fact that Sheckley's name appears twice on it. That is, if you almost never write any other kind of story but the one-puncher, the reader will come to expect nothing else of you, and will be ahead of you so often because of this subconscious preparation that he may decide to give up reading your material altogether. ⁄For whatever reason—perhaps not this one at all—Sheckley's popularity did suffer a near-disastrous slump not much later; and he is now rebuilding it on an entirely different foundation, beginning with a superb—and most complex—psychological novel, *The Man in the Water.*⁄ Still a second sub-class is the way in which habitual one-punch writing can creep into longer work. While I started out speaking of one-punchers purely as short stories, there are no less than three stories on the list which are classified by their editors as novelettes—"Watchbird" is one—and mighty thin novelettes they are.

Finally, there is the obvious danger of not writing a story at all. A writer sufficiently enamored of a single idea is quite capable of letting that idea carry the entire load. This is what happens in "Secret," which not only has no plot but succeeds in taking its faceless characters even farther away from the reader by presenting them through the medium of a transcribed investigation. We have already mentioned "Stamp from Moscow," which shares this scarcely minor flaw.

Nothing is ever going to drive the one-idea story out of science fiction, or for that matter out of any other field of fiction. There is no good reason why a one-idea story cannot also be a good story, *providing that* the idea is introduced to us in the beginning and the story is built around its consequences in terms of human beings. The one-punch story is, instead, a single, specialized,

*This particular piece of beard-muttering, I have since concluded, is almost diagnostic of the story which the author knows full well has a large logical hole in it, to which he is trying to blind you.

37

WILLIAM ATHELING, JR.

technical category of the one-idea story, wherein the story's only idea is hoarded jealously to be sprung on the reader as a (the author fondly hopes) surprise at the very end. It is almost always an unholy bore in any kind of fiction, and I do not exempt from this stricture the biggest bore of them all, O. Henry. And the one-punch story is probably a more serious miscalculation in science fiction than it is anywhere else. How often, after all, do you see a new idea in science fiction which is surprising of itself? Almost never, it seems to me; science fiction readers have had new ideas pulled out of the hat routinely since before 1928, and that "new" gimmick that the young writer plans to wow us with will turn out, nine chances to one, to have appeared at least five times before.

And this after all is the situation in which, in the long run, all fiction finds itself. The writer of short stories for the layman who swore that he wouldn't produce a line unless he had a truly new and original idea would wind up with a severe case of something closely resembling calf stifles.* What counts in the long run is not the idea but the point of view the writer brings to it— in other words, the set of additional ideas which the writer thinks appropriate to associate with it, a set which will vary almost completely from the one a second author would bring to bear on it. This is what editors mean when they talk about "fresh treatment." The one-punch story is no treatment at all, but simply an evasion.

Failure to grapple thoroughly with the logical consequences of an idea is one of the most common flaws in science fiction, as it is in all fiction. As a matter of fact, it occurs in almost all the arts, so that it is perfectly possible to draw comparisons between science fiction writers and composers, if you are interested in the broad question of how people grapple with aesthetic problems generally. A writer like van Vogt, for example, never really comes to grips with an idea, but just piles another one on top of it—this being exactly the procedure of all the major Russian composers from Glinka to Shostakovich. In the magazines for the quarter—to be specific, in *Galaxy* for February, 1953—we have a sample of the contrary tradition, the German symphonic development tradition, in which two strong but contrasting ideas are developed at length and to their logical conclusions, each

---

*Atheling asleep again. The stifle is not a disease of the calf, as I carelessly guessed, but an anatomical part.

one aided by the light the other casts on it. (For those of you who are trying to worry concrete points about writing from this book, this is mighty woolly talk, without doubt, but it won't do you any harm to think for a moment about writing as an art which exists in the same universe with other arts.) The story I refer to is "Four in One," by Damon Knight, whose knowledge of the craft that goes into good writing has been mentioned before. Note that the major idea in this story is not only as old as Homer, but has been handled before by science fiction writers of stature: the Proteus, the creature which can assume any shape. Knight makes no attempt to surprise anybody with this notion; even had he himself never encountered the idea before outside his own head, he is too good a craftsman to assume that an idea alone is enough. The contrasting idea is that of escape from a totalitarian society, again a piece of common coin. The result is "Four in One," which is compelling not because it contains a single new notion but because nobody but Knight ever before showed these two old notions in such an individual light, and because, in addition, the light is individual throughout—the story contains hardly a single stock reaction.

In contrast, "Null-ABC," the two-part serial by H. Beam Piper and John J. McGuire, which ran in *Astounding,* February and March, 1953 offers an idea which is new in detail if not in essence, and after an excellent start suddenly stops trying to do anything with it. There will probably be plenty of debate /there wasn't/ over the dim view these two authors take of present-day trends in education below the college level—I am inclined to think that they overstate a good case, which is almost a basic technique of all speculative or extrapolative fiction and not always a failing —but we can safely leave that debate to the letter columns. /Today we couldn't; only a few such columns survive./

From the point of view of technique, the story is most interesting for the way in which the authors abruptly abandon exploring their idea to take refuge in a cops-and-robbers plot (with a crew of Boy Adventurers thrown in for good measure). There is nothing in the battle of the department store, which occupies the entire last installment of the two, which depends logically from the proposition that literacy can become a universal stigma; it is just a battle, which would have been fought in about the same way regardless of the central proposition of the story. This, in contrast to "Four in One," is a stock reaction.

39

WILLIAM ATHELING, JR.

Just how stock it is I had not realized until, during this same quarter, I watched four horrible weeks of the *Captain Video* television show, putting on a script by Bryce Walton. Every night for ten nights running, Walton had an inoffensive character named Craig knocked down, sometimes twice in the same episode. After the author got tired of that, Craig knocked two other people down for the next two nights. No reason was given; it was action, wasn't it?*

The final major item for this period is also a serial, and one containing more than the usual quota of violence. It is "Police Your Planet," signed Erik van Lhin, which began in the March, 1953 issue of *Science Fiction Adventures*. I haven't yet seen the end of the novel, though I did read on into the next quarter in hopes of being able to render a judgment on the whole, but as of now I'm prepared to say that Mr. van Lhin, whoever he may be,● merits your close if somewhat cautious attention. For one thing, he appears to be intent upon importing into science fiction a tradition quite new to the field, although very old outside it, called naturalism. I happen to dislike this tradition intensely, but only as a matter of personal preference—it is a thoroughly respectable and important one and deserves to be explored.

Briefly, Erik van Lhin has set up a social situation on Mars which, while it resembles in some respects the social hells in which the novels of Zola, Farrell, and other naturalists take place, is markedly a science fiction situation, depending upon a set of extrapolations rather than upon a simple transfer of present-day situations to the future and to another planet. Having done this, he then proceeds to tell you in plain, flat terms just what this situation would mean for the people who have to live in it. The result is gruesome, but it seems to me that it is generally honest and thorough, with only as many stock reactions as you would expect in naturalistic writing.

*Not long afterward, I had the chance of writing three weeks of the show. I too used Craig, but nobody hit him and he hit nobody, though my scripts were otherwise pretty melodramatic. No complaints were reported.

●Erik van Lhin—as I was lucky enough to figure out before the last installment of "Police Your Planet" appeared—was one of science fiction's masters, Lester del Rey, who was also at the time the editor of the magazine. He wrote the novel an installment at a time, just in time to squeeze each into the magazine. All three of these facts provide illuminating hindsights on Atheling's bafflement at being confronted with a novel at once so startling and so flawed, by a writer he'd never heard of. They may also explain why my copy of the hard-bound version of the novel (Avalon, 1956) is inscribed to "Atheling" by "van Lhin" as a book "which would have been dedicated to him if it had been the book I wanted it to be."

Since most of even these stock reactions will be totally un-familiar to most science fiction readers, the resulting story—as far as it has gone—is that rare object, a real shocker. Many readers will hate it passionately, for it has more plain squalor and less romance than any science fiction story I know, including *1984*. But the squalor, the violence, the vice, and indeed all the elements of the story spring directly from a dreadful situation honestly imagined and honestly carried through; and if the result is dreadful (emotionally, not technically), it is a tribute to the man who wrote it that way. I cannot imagine anyone enjoying this story for its content, but as craftsmanship it is open to considerable admiration.

A certain number of relatively unpleasant subjects have seemed ready to sneak into science fiction during the past few years. One of them, normal sexual relationships, actually has become accepted by all but the incurable vestal virgins among us, and some readers are now ready to admit that the subject isn't so unpleasant after all. Murder, of course, hasn't been an unpleasant subject for decades. Alfred Bester, in *The Demolished Man* (Shasta, 1953), buried a number of highly sarcastic jokes on more or less taboo subjects—among the neatest of these being a minor character who was a blind voyeur. And in "Big Planet" (*Startling Stories*, September, 1952) Jack Vance actually went so far as to state that if the heroine really was raped before the hero could rescue her, it wouldn't be too serious an event. You can probably add a fair list of such dying taboos.

The van Lhin novel takes the opposite tack. It assumes that you share the common feeling that rape is a peculiarly horrible crime, and it even assumes that murder is a horrible crime too, which of course it is; and the author then proceeds relentlessly to exacerbate your feelings in these matters, until you begin to wonder if the Earth will ever be clean before the last human being is exterminated. It is a humorless and limited performance, but a compelling one, as naturalistic writing always is because it is so easily believable; the reader can so easily see himself in what he reads, and half of his horror springs from his own sense of self-knowledge. Let words of praise be spoken for van Lhin, and for del Rey behind his false whiskers as Philip St. John (under which pen-name he edited the magazine).

Both men should be warned, however, that if this novel ends in a burst of hope and glory, as all but the best of this breed in-

WILLIAM ATHELING, JR.

variably do, I shall have strong words to say about the forever-impenetrable wall between fiction and propaganda. /Well, it did and it didn't. Try it yourself, preferably in the magazine version if you can find it. The hardback is much abridged, and not by the author.7

Minor and personal note: I hope you were touched, as I was, by Theodore Sturgeon's "Saucer of Loneliness" *(Galaxy*, February, 1953). You should not let the clumsy title put you off. Technically the piece is quite perfect, which makes it extraordinary to begin with. It is open to cavil on the grounds of personal taste because of its burgeoning sentimentality, which some readers may find as impossible to like as I find van Lhin's implacable sequence of ugly acts and motives—but it has to be accepted on exactly the same grounds. While neither story is in the least cerebral, but instead makes a concentrated and probably calculated assault upon the emotions, it is precisely to the cerebrum that both stories appeal as technical achievements, and hence succeed in impressing upon the reader two different sets of values which he probably could not understand or even agree with temporarily.*

And as for the question of what constitutes a new idea, what could be more hackneyed these days than the flying saucer? Yet out of that stale notion Ted has wrung a deeply personal story, one which will probably be remembered much longer than stories like Heinlein's "The Puppet Masters" *(Galaxy*, September/November, 1951), where flying saucers appear only because they were in the news when the author was writing the story, and appear in a form the audience assumes that they take.

Ideas alone lead nowhere. Only ideas about ideas make good fiction, as they make good music, or good science, or for that matter good living.

---

*I do not fault this judgment of the Sturgeon story ten years later, but just this once I shall have to second-guess Atheling. "Saucer of Loneliness," like an earlier and scarifying story by Eric Frank Russell ("I Am Nothing," <u>Astounding</u>, July, 1952), turned out to be simply a retelling of a touching anecdote widely reported in the press, to which the science fiction trappings were not contributory; on the contrary, they were distracting. In short, Sturgeon's story violated Sturgeon's Definition: It was space opera.

A Sprig of Editors *Summer, 1953*

IN THE YEARS PRIOR TO THE DELUGE
⌈of professional science fiction magazines, now long dry⌋, Hal
Clement's article "Whirligig World" (*Astounding*, June, 1953)
probably would have appeared only in a fan magazine. The article,
a brief piece with diagrams, deals with the preliminary work
which went into the writing of "Mission of Gravity," the four-part
serial which ran in the magazine, April through July. The initial
paper-work for this serial, as you might expect from a writer of
Clement's thoroughness, was extensive and careful, and it is
probably largely responsible for the tone of authority and conviction the novel itself conveys. The story is, in my opinion, the
only noteworthy serial *Astounding* has run in years.

At the moment, the most interesting thing about the article is
that it was run in the magazine proper at all. Formally, it conveys little information that can't be found in the story: it is a
sort of *Omnibook* digest of the background and setting of "Mission
of Gravity." What additional information it does include is classi-
fiable as gossip (such as the fact that Isaac Asimov offered a
hand in working out the chemistry of Mesklin). Aside from the
formal content, however, it tells us a number of things about
Astounding, about science fiction writers and editors under the
conditions prevailing on today's market, and about present-day
readers, not all of which make pleasant reading-between-the-lines.

Perhaps the most obvious deduction we can make about the
publication of this piece is that of Campbell's reason for wanting
to print it. Campbell has been in the field so long that most of

us are aware of his admiration for elaborately worked-out story
backgrounds. The history of this preference runs from the days
when he publicly admired a minor facet of a story—by Gallun, as
I recall—because it had taken JWCjr eight pages of calculation
to confirm it, through the days of the outsize *Astounding* when
Campbell was telling us that he was encouraging longer stories
because they made for a more "lived-in" world of the future, to
the present publication of Clement's article. This is the first
time within my memory, however, that Campbell has actually
printed a How-Dun-It by one of his major writers—and it seems
to me to follow that the article was commissioned, since, with no
precedent available, Clement would hardly have been likely to
have written such an article on speculation. (Not, at least, for
JWCjr, but that simply makes the proposition more unlikely, for
since when has Campbell been buying articles originally intended
for *Skyhook?)*

Why does Campbell want his readers to know that writing a
long science fiction story takes careful preparation before the
more obviously fictional elements of the story are filled in?
First, because he assumes that his readers don't know it. In
itself this is a revolutionary assumption. There was a time in
the development of magazine science fiction when the most vocal
part of the readership insisted upon minute attention to detail,
and as much accuracy as the known facts of a given case would
permit. This is not a prejudice fostered by Campbell. It was
implicit in T. O'Conor Sloane's delight in listing every degree
and academic honor his authors (or he himself) had ever earned,
up to and including some esoteric British society memberships
which must have puzzled most of the Teck *Amazing's* readers in
Britain alone. It was equally visible in Gernsback's practice,
and in Gernsback's last magazine, *Science Fiction Plus,* the
emphasis upon the scientific qualifications of the authors was
even more nakedly paraded, and sometimes even more dishonestly.
Everybody once knew that to be a good science fiction writer you

*I probably ought to note that Clement has been known to do this kind of thing for fun.
At the 18th World Science Fiction Convention (Pittsburgh, 1959), for instance, he described a
solar system he had designed in which it would be physically possible for heroes and villains
to flit casually from planet to planet, as they impossibly do in most swashbuckling space opera.
This came complete with two three-dimensional models and a detailed descriptive booklet
("Some Notes on Xi Bootis"; published as a free souvenir of the convention by Advent: Publishers), and since, Clement said, he felt he wasn't a good swashbuckler as a writer, he threw
the system open for the rest of us. Nobody has yet taken him up on the offer; swashbucklers
mostly don't give a damn.

had to Know Your Science, and when a man was once reported to have bragged that he got all the science he knew out of a pint bottle of Scotch, he was a sport spoken of, more often than not, with affectionate contempt.

Something, evidently, has happened to this assumption since the new boom began. Campbell visibly has decided that his present readership needs to be told that good science fiction writers try to be reasonably accurate and consistent in their handling of scientific materials. The next question is, what part of his readership? Most of his flock of faithful are already aware of the fact, whether they continue to care greatly about it or not (and we presume they do, or *Astounding* would have a new editor). As for the new readers, does Campbell believe he can convert a substantial number of those who are not sold on the point already —and read his magazine in preference to, say, *Galaxy,* because they slightly prefer accuracy above smooth writing? And if he does convert the remaining minority, what has he gained?

Clement's article, it becomes increasingly evident, is addressed primarily to *Astounding's writers*—not only the past and present stables, but that possible stable in the immediate future. I at least can imagine no other pressure which could have resulted in the publication of this fan-magazine piece in *Astounding*. Campbell believes, like many of us still, that a certain deference to what is already known or is conceivable from already-known facts is important to science fiction; and he is not now getting it from his writers, by and large. He has just given his writers public notice of the fact, and has published an example of what he thinks *ought* to be done by a science fiction writer before he undertakes a seriously intended science fiction story.

Whether or not this is already a losing battle remains to be seen. There are plenty of divisions on the other side. Nearly every new magazine which appears on the stands these days has the same self-justification to offer on this question: The editors say they believe that science fiction was once, or has become, too technical, and what they are going to offer by God is *entertainment;* nor is this a new notion, for it was the Merwin-Mines line for years, and it has many partisans. It reached some kind of apotheosis recently in a Kendell Foster Crossen editorial appealing to readers (read: writers) to "throw the science out of science fiction." One can sympathize with Mr. Crossen, whose knowledge of any science could hardly be used to stop a mouse-

45

WILLIAM ATHELING, JR.

hole, and whose survival in the field depends upon readers who
think chlorophyll is a Wonder Drug, but one could stop at sympathy
were it not so patent that Mr. Crossen speaks for an increasing
number of readers and writers in this field.

To be sure, the story's the thing. There Mr. Crossen and
confreres are indubitably in the right of it. The purists (among
whom I list myself) have long ago lost this battle, simply because
the anti-science boys had the great good fortune to have an artist
on their side. The story is the thing; Bradbury writes stories,
and usually remarkable ones; he is of course a scientific blind-
worm, but in the face of such artistry, it's difficult to care. Most
writers, I think, would be happy to grant Bradbury this—and
would be equally glad to grant it to anyone else in Crossen's
camp who could show something like the same deference for
writing as a serious thing in itself. This was the major difficulty
with the old anti-science writers, such as the younger Hamilton,
who not only did not care whether or not their facts were accurate,
but displayed an equally manifest contempt for the craft of writing
as a whole. Probably, I would add, Mr. Bradbury did us good: In
the heyday of the scientifically accurate story, bus-bars often
got substituted for plots, and more generally speaking respect
for facts went hand in hand with ignorance of writing.* As I say,
the purists have lost that battle, and everybody benefits by the
loss.

If, however, the respect for facts is now to be swamped out,
nobody is likely to win, least of all the reader. This respect is
fundamental to fiction, not just science fiction alone, but all fiction.
Once the observed fact goes—whether it's an observation on the
breathability of the atmosphere of Mars, or an observation on
what a human being (not a child, a robot, or an imaginary alien)
might do in a given situation—the writer can no longer be trusted;
he is not looking at the universe around him, but simply into his
liver. And if the reader is encouraged to think of this kind of
writing—which is not even self-examination in the Socratic sense,
any more than keeping a record of the amount of lint one's umbili-
cus accumulates between baths is self-examination—as the utmost
he should ask from his authors, he will find himself at last with

*or, as Longfellow put it:
        Street is real and Smith is earnest;
        Harry Stine is not our goal.
         Audel's Handy Wiring Manual
        Does not satisfy the soul.

nobody to read but Janifers: writers who respect neither the craft nor the materials used by the craft.

I have been hoping for some time now to remark briefly on the surprisingly good job Robert W. Lowndes has been making of his three Columbia publications, *Dynamic, Future,* and *Science Fiction Quarterly.* For those who do not know the financial facts that obtain about these /now extinct/ magazines, Lowndes' showing may not seem so unexpected, since he is a man of intelligence and taste and has personal friendships with almost every major writer in the business. Unhappily, however, it works for a publishing house which seems to operate on the theory that if writers are not paid until they ask for payment, they just may forget to ask entirely. (It still operates in this way.) There is a legend in the editorial offices at Columbia that Cyril Kornbluth once did exactly this. Furthermore, Columbia's rates are rock-bottom, falling in some instances below the one-cent-per-word mark. This is nothing new with Columbia, either—Low and Slow has been the payment motto there for at least a decade.

Under these circumstances, no editor no matter how competent could expect to get any stories in his mail but those that have been rejected by everybody else in sight, and it's difficult to operate a magazine one can respect out of the slush-pile. That Lowndes succeeds in operating three which, though erratic, remain pretty consistently readable and occasionally contain genuine surprises is therefore no mean achievement. He uses three techniques: one, he squeezes money from the back of the book to pay higher rates for the front of it; two, he makes use (quite legitimately, let me add) of the fact that a number of well-known authors are close personal friends to commission stories from these people, a feat he could never pull off at his rates under any other circumstances; and last, he appears to read his slush-pile right down to the ground, with a sharp eye for possible new talents. (All editors *say* they do this, of course, but Lowndes *has* to do it to maintain his present level of performance. No non-editor can appreciate the eyestrain and the patience involved in such a policy.)

The slightly higher rates for lead stories gives him the assurance that he will see stories by known writers somewhere near the halfway point of the manuscripts' travels, rather than at the end—hence, apparently, the excellent lead yarns by Jack

WILLIAM ATHELING, JR.

Vance and Cyril Judd (Cyril Kornbluth and Judith Merril) which he has run recently. The commissions produce more uneven work, partly since most of them are written around already-painted covers, but most of the surprises come from this category: in *Future*, January, 1953 for instance, there was an experimental yarn called "Testament of Andros" by James Blish, which almost certainly was too off-beat to have been sold to or even written for any other editor. (The yarn, told in five distinctly different styles by five narrators who may or may not have been the same man, was in my opinion too big a job for its author, but it was well worth attempting.) And the close reading of the slush pile, though it is probably as hard on the digestion as it is on the eye, has resulted in several coups: for example, Lowndes was one of the first editors to run a story by Robert Sheckley, in the days before that prolific youngster had either reputation or sales record, or even so much as an agent.

Of course the magazines are erratic. Not even Lowndes could totally combat the effects of Columbia's Low and Slow payment policy, and in addition, like all of us, Lowndes has blind spots—among which might be listed his fascination by the pedestrian, out-at-the-elbows prose of Walter Kubilius, who so persistently runs last in Lowndes' own readers' ratings as to make one wonder if this is not a case of friendship run amok. On the whole, however, the editorial standards being applied here are consistently intelligent and pegged far higher than a lesser editor would consider justified by the budget. It is an instructive exercise to compare them with those of such an editor as Howard Browne, who in spite of an egregious display of comparative wealth can seldom bring himself to buy a bad story if he has a worse one on hand.

About THREE DECADES AGO—MORE or less coinciding with the first of the great theism-vs.-atheism arguments to rage in the letter columns of the professional magazines—H. P. Lovecraft remarked (in *Supernatural Horror in Literature*, Abramson, 1945) that it was futile to attempt to describe possible peoples of other planets simply by exporting to them wholesale the folk customs of Earth. One of the folk customs listed by HPL in the course of his comment was royalty; another was religion.

It is perfectly obvious, of course, that the "alien princess" of *Planet Stories* and Edgar Rice Burroughs is nothing more than a trope, and a long-dead one at that (though reviewers for such journals as *Time* and *The Saturday Review of Nothing* have yet to notice the fact). It is not quite so self-evident that we will not find gods, or the belief in them, on other planets. We find them everywhere on Earth, which cannot be said of royalty or the other folk customs mentioned by Lovecraft; and even where we do not find specific deities, we find religion's immediate precursor, magic.

A case could be made, I think, for the proposition that any humanly conceivable thinking creature will arrive at magic, and hence eventually at religion in some form, before he can arrive at scientific method, since the basic proposition of the one is, in essence, a less precise form of the other. The root assumption of sympathetic magic, as any reader of Pratt/de Camp (or Frazer) already knows, is "Similar actions produce similar results."

WILLIAM ATHELING, JR.

The root assumption of scientific method might be stated in the same form: "Identical actions produce identical results." The difference between the two assumptions, aside from the fact that the first does not work and the second does, is a matter of refinement of observation—and it is difficult to accept that any thinking creature, no matter how bug-eyed or many-tentacled, could so evolve as to arrive at the more precise formulation first. He may, of course, have since outgrown the earlier faith, as we have not, but nevertheless traces of it would almost surely remain buried in his culture.

Whether or not you accept this proposition, however—and there are doubtless many anthropocentric assumptions in it—we can at least be sure that man will export his own gods into space, as surely as he exports his languages, his nationalisms, and his belief in his own rationality. Science fiction has already dealt at some length with the problems of interplanetary man's allegiance to a home country, to a government, to the family he left behind, and even to the home sexual code. Lately there have been several science-fictional inquiries into his relationship with the home god—as distinguished from the local gods, such as the one Heinlein's "Methuselah's Children" (*Astounding,* July/September, 1941) ran afoul of.

This is of peculiar interest to the practising writer or critic, be he theist or mechanistic materialist himself, because it represents an enormous potential extension of the subject matter of science fiction in the direction of real human problems—which is the direction in which the medium must be extended if it is to remain viable. You may feel, for instance, as Arthur C. Clarke does, that to carry national boundaries into space would be to export a primitive superstition which it would be criminal to continue on other worlds than ours—yet the chances are good that we will export this folk custom, along with our penchant for killing each other and many similar quaint, un-idealistic practices. By the same token, like it or not, a real human being sitting in a real lunar crater is more than likely to be spending a certain proportion of his time wondering whether or not the god of his fathers is with him yet—and using his decisions on this subject as bases for action. The science fiction writer can no more ignore this than he can the probable extension of nationalism into space. It is one of the ways that human beings think, a way so basic that it involves their emotions as well. As such, it is

50

not only a proper but a fertile subject for fiction of any kind, and science fiction in particular.

These remarks arise primarily out of several re-readings of "A Case of Conscience," by James Blish (*If*, September, 1953), an exhaustive and occasionally exhausting study of a Roman Catholic priest thrown into an ethical and theological dilemma by what he finds on a new planet. Almost the whole text of the story, which runs to about 25,000 words, is devoted to the problem, its background, its implications, the lines of reasoning involved in making a decision, and the nature of the decision itself. Though several things "happen," there is no action as such in the yarn, and most of the drama is dialectical. Part of the length of the story is contributed by sheer physical description of the planet, in which the author indulges so extensively as to delay telling the reader the story's central problem until he is nearly two thirds of the way through it—and probably losing two thirds of his readers in the process; but the detail, as it turns out, is valuable, first because it establishes a slow and discursive tone *before* the reader is plunged into the elaborate four-way argument which is the essence of the piece, and second because most of the details (though not all) are integral to the argument itself.

What the general reader of science fiction will make of this story is still an unanswered question,* and in my judgment an important one—not only because of the subject matter, which is not as novel as editor Shaw's promotional smokescreen would lead you to believe, but also because of its narrative technique, which is unique in my experience. My initial impression was that readers who enjoy what Poe called "ratiocination" for its own sake, and who in addition could suspend their own prejudices about the subject matter long enough to feel Father Ruiz' dilemma as acutely as he himself felt it, would find the story intensely exciting, while everyone else would yawn and look baffled. Then I remembered G. K. Chesterton's Father Brown stories, where there is also considerable display of straight reasoning, plus a uniformly religious point of view brought to bear upon the problems of a specialized idiom (in this case, the detective story). Conceivably, "A Case of Conscience" is well enough told as a story to carry a similar general appeal; although intricate, it is

*See the Afterword to this essay.

51

WILLIAM ATHELING, JR.

anything but incoherent, and it is so paced—as I've noted above —as to make the final argument seem highly dramatic, in the face of the obvious obstacles to such an impression. Furthermore, several other attitudes toward the religious problem are represented by other characters in the story, so that, although the author obviously intended the reader to identify himself with Father Ruiz' point of view, he has provided handles for dissidents to grasp if they will.

This took considerable doing. I have made no secret of the fact that I mistrust the average reader's ability to weigh technical competence, or even to recognize it, so that I can make no present assessment of the effectiveness of what Blish has done here; theoretically he should have captured his audience, even though most of it will not know why it is captured or how the trick was turned. On the other hand, he may have captured nobody but a cross-section of other writers who are in a position to appreciate how much work this kind of story takes, without being any better able to weigh its effectiveness with a non-technical reader than I am. (In any group of experts, the incidence of a disease called "expertitis," the major symptom of which is a perverse delight in talking over the heads of the rabble, is invariably high. In our field, even Damon Knight shows touches of it now and then, and Atheling was permanently put to bed of it long ago.) The question is somewhat clouded, furthermore, by several direct failures of technique in the Blish story, so that if the yarn as a whole fails to communicate, it will be hard to tell whether (a) it failed because the techniques we think most effective are really of little value, (b) it failed because these techniques, though valuable enough, were not well enough realized in this story, or (c) it failed because no conceivable attention to technique could prevail against the novelty and the touchiness of the story's subject matter. If it succeeds, of course, the same questions remain to be answered.

Insofar as evidence exists on point (c), it seems safe to say that novelty and touchiness of subject matter probably will not seriously affect the verdict. The subject matter of "A Case of Conscience" is still unusual in our field, but it is no longer strange. As I noted at the beginning of this essay, the extension of science fiction story problems into this realm has now become quite marked, so that Blish's story is not a freak but part of a trend. It is perhaps not quite an accident that one of the earliest and best of such science fiction stories, Hugh Benson's *Lord of the World* (Dodd, Mead, 1908), was called to fandom's attention by Virginia Kidd, then Blish's wife—and that Benson, like Blish's Father Ruiz, was a Jesuit. (Father Benson also wrote a sequel to the novel, of which Miss Kidd was apparently unaware.) The wildly, floridly spooky M. P. Shiel charged into the arena, exclamation points shooting in all directions, with his 1901 novel *Lord of the Sea* (and it is ridiculous but characteristic of Sam Moskowitz to call the book anti-Semitic; the book's subject is the polities of Zionism, and its climax the advent of the Messiah; but of course style-deaf people who think books about Jews should contain no Jewish villains had better be restricted to Peter Rabbit anyhow). The interplanetary novels of C. S. Lewis (*Out of the Silent Planet, Perelandra,* and *That Hideous Strength*) offer more recent examples; they set out to impose upon the solar system a strange Anglican-cum-Babylonian theology and cosmogony, with amazingly convincing results despite Lewis' decidedly foggy view of astronomy and most of the other sciences he seeks to diabolize.

The first notable stirrings of religious interest in the magazines during the 1950 science fiction boom probably can be traced back to Ray Bradbury's "The Man" (*Thrilling Wonder Stories,* February, 1949), a parable of the Second Coming of Christ. I have mentioned this before, because it has been the subject of considerable imitation; but it is also interesting because it proposes that Christ is traveling from planet to planet with his Message, a project which will take Him forever and hence reduces Bradbury's intended devoutness to a numerical absurdity by proposing that an omnipotent God can arrange a multiple Advent only seriatim, by turning His Son into the Wandering Salesman. (The Messiah of the Jews, be it noted, is under no such limitation; he can turn up everywhere at once, like Santa Claus, and indeed this doctrine is specifically celebrated in Judaism's children's festival.) A much more sensitive short story by one of *Planet's* former editors, Paul L. Payne ("Fool's Errand," *Thrilling Wonder Stories,* October, 1952), dealt with an attempt to hoax a devout Jewish member of the first spaceship crew to Mars, by planting a phony cross on the planet; it fails because the hoaxer's boot also sheds a nail on the site of the plant, a coincidence which the Jewish spaceman is too hard-headed to accept, though it

WILLIAM ATHELING, JR.

would have thrown most Sunday Christians into paroxysms of easy superstition. (And not just Protestants, either; think what the Fatima-worshippers would have made of such a juncture, despite all that the Devil's Advocates could possibly try to discourage them.)

The pattern that begins to emerge here—and I have selected only a few of many possible examples—is a startling one. Before I put a name to it, let me call to your attention what these writers are talking about, underneath the science-fictional trappings, the easy gestures and the Sunday sentimentality. Putting "A Case of Conscience" aside for the moment because we have thus far considered only half of it, we find Father Benson talking about the coming of the Anti-Christ; Shiel about the coming of the Messiah; Lewis about the coming of the Next Sacrifice (Ransom), the magical Messiah (Merlin), and the Anti-Christ (his scientist-villain who turns into Satan in *Perelandra,* and anti-climactically into H. G. Wells in *That Hideous Strength*); Bradbury and his imitators about Christ the Wandering Salesman, scorned by His audiences (thus combining the Anti-Christ legend and the Flying Dutchman); and Payne about the human agent of a false Messiah, who is seen through easily by a Jew to whom "Messias ist *nicht* gekommen" has been an article of faith since 2 A.D.

Now, I think, we know more exactly what it is that we are considering here. These science fiction stories are not fundamentally theological at all. Every one of them, including "Case" and some others I am about to cite, are instead instruments of a chiliastic crisis, of a magnitude we have not seen since the world-wide chiliastic panic of 999 A.D., when everyone expected the Second Coming and the Last Judgment on the next New Year's Morning, and nobody in his heart of hearts could bring himself to believe in the forgiveness of Christ. We no more believe in it now than we did then, and small wonder; and our modern Apocalyptic literature, overlaid though it is with the mythologies of scientific humanism and heroid technology, takes just as dim a view of it.

One science fiction story about religion which at first glance does not seem to fit this definition is Anthony Boucher's "The Quest for Saint Aquin," which was written for Raymond J. Healy's 1951 anthology, *New Tales of Space and Time* (Holt). This piece dealt with the soul-struggles of a post-atom-war Catholic priest

54

against a robot tempter, while in search of a saint who also turned out to be a robot. But the story about atomic Armageddon and the post-bomb world is almost by definition apocalyptic—and to reinforce the tie, Mr. Boucher has it that Aquin, being a perfectly logical machine, is *therefore* a Roman Catholic, thus providing a Second Coming complete with the presently fashionable Neo-Thomism. (One wonders what St. Thomas would have thought of this; after all, the legend tells us that he smashed Albertus Magnus' magical brass head for getting the better of him in an argument.)

Incidentally, Boucher remarked of his story, in the preface to the book, that it "could almost certainly never have appeared in any magazine in the field" because of its theme. If this was so at the time—and it probably was—the appearance of Blish's story in *If* affords a rough measurement of the progress of the trend in two years. ("Case" did not get into print initially without some resistance, however—Horace Gold of *Galaxy* offered to take it only if "there's some way we can get rid of this religious jazz —I run a family magazine." Happily, both Shaw of *If* and Lester del Rey of *Space Science Fiction* wanted it, Shaw without conditions, del Rey on the promise of a sequel.)

All the elements of the Boucher story appear writ large in Walter M. Miller, Jr.'s deservedly admired novel *A Canticle for Leibowitz* (Lippincott, 1960), which was foreshadowed by a moving Miller short story, "Crucifixus Etiam" (*Astounding*, February, 1953), and which itself originally appeared as a series of magazine short stories. Several commentators, Boucher in particular, have called attention to the fact that almost all science fiction stories dealing with religion assume a Roman Catholic frame, and that this cannot entirely be explained by assuming that the authors are Catholics (Blish is a professed agnostic; Bradbury and Payne are not on record, but their texts show no doctrinal commitments). This observation ceases to be puzzling, however, the moment one realizes that the stories all seek to express, or perhaps sometimes exploit, a common chiliastic panic, so that the choice of the most complex, best organized and oldest body of Christian dogma as an intellectual background seems only natural. Only the always sportive Shiel made another choice, which emerged naturally from the fact that he was writing about a *First* Coming (though he rather clouds the issue in the last few pages of the novel with a sort of Christian psalm). He was, of course, pre-Bomb; so was Benson, but he was a priest.*

So much for precedents. The major difference between all these stories and "A Case of Conscience" is simply technical, not philosophical. It lies in the deliberate avoidance of anything which could wear the name of action, or, to put it positively, in an intensive concentration upon dialectic as the major story-telling device. For the most part, I think it successful; but such single-mindedness often runs to excess, and this story is no exception. It is necessarily a talky story, but it probably did not need to be so damned talky; the long conversation between Ruiz and Chtexa which falls immediately after the yarn's best cliff-hanger, for instance, drags on beyond the merely suspenseful into the maddening, and could have been cut nearly in half to the story's profit. The huge mass of detail and local color is also overdone: when it deals with such integral features of the local landscape as the Message Tree, it justifies itself, and the detailed discussion of the local method of reproduction is essential to the main argument—but the descriptions also include long catalogues of the local raw materials, discussions of the weather, and similar dead or at least indifferent matter which would overbalance any story of this length, even one as slow-paced as this one obviously needed to be. (Expertitis again?)

Finally—and this may well be the oddest complaint I ever have to make about a story—the ending of "A Case of Conscience" fails to be ambiguous enough. It is intended to leave the whole question posed by the story up in the air, for the reader to answer as best he can, but instead Blish traps himself in a piece of elementary symbolism which can easily be taken to imply a ready-made answer. I refer to the business of Cleaver's crates, which so dominates Ruiz' final dialogue with Chtexa as to suggest that Cleaver may be preparing to blow up the ship in mid-space, or otherwise tamper with the evidence. The falling of Cleaver's shadow over Ruiz' in the airlock, and the slamming of the airlock door ("Cleaver's trademark") reinforces the impression that it is Cleaver's point of view which will win in the long run, an im-

*I find that Jungian analysts share my view that fear of the Bomb is the modern version of the 999 riots, and that Jung himself notes that the religious character of the flying saucer cults is based specifically on a hope that the Saucerites are going to Save us; one such cult even maintains that Christ was born on Venus, which makes the Earth just another of Bradbury's way-stations for the Wandering Salesman. I quite agree, but I wish I could rid myself of the suspicion that Jung himself thinks the saucers to be real.

pression which is totally false to the story as I read it.

In the meantime, religion, like science, is certainly doing its best to catch up with science fiction. "A Case of Conscience" includes a speculation that the creatures of other planets may never die, because, never having been in the Garden of Eden in the first place, they may not be considered by God as subject to the Curse of Adam. The identical speculation was making the rounds of the Vatican at the time the story was published (only a revival, of course; the problem of "the plurality of worlds" was not precisely new when Galileo inconveniently made it seem acute). The feeling is shared, furthermore, by many people with no sectarian axe to grind; I quote the July, 1953 issue of *The Journal of the British Interplanetary Society* (p. 178): "One day a landing on the moon will be made....One would like to think that amid all the technical jubilation somebody will get up and say: 'Remember! For the first time since Adam the slate is clean.'"

Afterword *1964*

Looking at a story of one's own in this fashion is a difficult and perhaps a foredoomed exercise, and one impossible to free from suspicions of disingenuousness or outright dishonesty (of which I was duly accused at least once). Nevertheless, I'm glad I tried it; and in retrospect, it affords me the chance to check my critical performance in several ways that I couldn't have predicted and hence couldn't have attempted to set up for myself even had I wanted to.

That I did indeed capture some sort of audience is now established. The story brought me many letters, some from Catholics pointing out minor errors of ritual and dogma, some from militant atheists accusing me of being a Jesuit proselytizer, and all shades of opinion in between. It was anthologized only once, in England, but so dominated the other stories with which it appeared that reviews of the book barely mentioned most of them. The novel version (Ballantine, 1958)—not an expansion of the story, but a continuation of it, long after Lester del Rey had requested one—took the "Hugo" award for the best science fiction novel of 1958; in addition to its first American publication, it has seen three

WILLIAM ATHELING, JR.

British editions, plus one each in France, Italy, Brazil, and Japan; has been dramatized at Hardin-Simmons University, made the subject of a half-hour lecture on the BBC's *Third Programme,* and discussed almost endlessly almost everywhere. All this is doubly gratifying when I remember that the night I finished the story, I predicted to my then wife that nobody would ever buy it (except Fletcher Pratt, who, having commissioned it for a Twayne anthology, was stuck with it).

The trend in subject matter which I predicted arrived and accelerated on schedule; so I have not hesitated to expand my 1953 remarks on that subject with a few more words I added nearly ten years later in Dick and Pat Lupoff's fan magazine *Xero.* As noted earlier, no credit is due me for this prediction anyhow, since the question of the plurality of worlds is an old one, and it was bound to arise once more as soon as spaceflight began to seem imminent to laymen as well as to science fiction readers. The distinction between the Apocalyptic and the chiliastic types emerged during the course of a recent all-night discussion with del Rey, and I don't think either of us could have arrived at it back in 1953, when there were still too few examples of religious science fiction to make the division evident. (Even del Rey's magnificently blasphemous Apocalyptic story, "For I Am a Jealous People," in *Star Short Novels,* Ballantine, 1954 was unwritten then, though he had been brooding about it earlier.)

The technical criticisms of the 1952 story still seem to me to be sound, if what we are talking about is still that story only. This must indeed be borne in mind, because at the time I wrote the criticism, I had no intention of writing a sequel, and had none in mind; the piece was supposed to be complete as it stood—and as such, I still think, it had the flaws I pointed out. When I was later afforded the chance to go on into novel length, I had the benefit of my own second thoughts, and I believe I used most of them.

For example, Atheling complains of the "catalogues of the local raw materials"; but eventually it becomes important to the story that one of these raw materials is amazingly abundant, whereas certain other more likely ones are very rare—and both these facts are buried in the catalogues, detective-story fashion, for the reader of the novel. Neither Atheling nor the author of the story were in a position to appreciate this a decade ago. Similarly, the heavy weighting of the end of the magazine story toward

58

Cleaver still seems inexcusable if the story is to stop there—but if the story is to go on, then it becomes a fine multiple cliff-hanger, making Ruiz' situation seem quite hopeless when the feel of the book in the reader's hands says plainly that there is more to come—indeed, more than half.

In fact, a curious effect of the novelization of the story is that it is now too short, although section one—the magazine story—was further expanded, and the new section is still longer than the first. Even at this length, there is just too much material there to escape an effect of breathlessness as the novel draws toward a close, and there was nothing I could do about it; at the time of writing, I was held by contract to 75,000 words, that being the largest book that Ballantine could then bind in the paperback format. Hence I am afraid that even today Atheling would find the completed work somewhat out of balance, though for reasons neither he nor I had anticipated.

Another Case *April, 1962*

Religious subjects are no longer entirely strange to the science fiction novel, and if we have many more which just skate along the surface, such novels may shortly fall prey to Gresham's Law. The danger is successfully skirted, though, in *Believers' World* by Robert Lowndes (Avalon, 1961). The book is a distinct oddity, and must have seemed even odder in 1952, when a drastically cut version of it appeared in one of Lester del Rey's magazines (as "A Matter of Faith" by Michael Sherman, *Space Science Fiction,* September, 1952); certainly it has had no successors.

There are actually three "believers' worlds" in the novel, each one run by a theocracy derived from teachings which are identical on all three worlds—yet each planet grimly maintains that the religions of the other two are heresies. Since each of the planets can destroy either of the others (but not both at once) at will, this makes for tight politics, to say the least.

The theological significance of all this is debatable and it's my guess that it's also quite minor. Primarily the book is a novel of action, with a plot of intrigue of awesome and perhaps un-

WILLIAM ATHELING, JR.

necessary complexity; and the secret of the religion of Ein turns out to be a Chinese-box joke-within-a-joke-within-a-joke, to which you may be tempted to respond, "Oh, not so *damned* shaggy!" When the novelette version first appeared, Atheling proposed that Lowndes might have been mocking the sterile version of Anglicanism epitomized in T. S. Eliot's famous line, "The spirit killeth, but the letter giveth life"—a precise description of what happens at the crisis of this novel. Lowndes denied it; I think the book version can also be read this way, whatever the author's intentions, but I won't insist.

What is more interesting is that this remains one of the very few science fiction works to exploit the world-view of Oswald Spengler, once an enormously popular philosopher historian, but now more deeply in eclipse than I think he should be.* Lowndes has used several major themes from Spengler in elaborate counterpoint.

The solar system of Ein is completely enclosed in a hyperspatial bubble which provides it with a time-rate much faster than that of our space—25 times as fast, in fact—but doesn't otherwise block passage between the three worlds and Earth. The effect is to bar any real exchange of knowledge between Earth and the Ein system, since nobody who spends enough time on Ein worlds to learn anything valuable can talk to his fellows when he gets back home.

However, Earthmen visiting the Ein worlds continue to be intelligible there because the whole culture has frozen. Earth was going through what Spengler calls a "pseudomorphosis" when the Ein system was colonized; that is, it was going through vast technological and other superficial changes which did not really alter its essential cultural stage; and the colonists partook of this disorientation. After their landings, the walled-off space and time of the Ein system jelled them into a "Magian" culture, contemporary (in Spengler's sense) with the abortive Arab culture of the ninth and the twelfth centuries A.D.; and there they are stuck, since physically their .space-time *actually* conforms to

---

*The first two published stories of A. E. van Vogt were explicitly Spenglerian—in fact the characters lectured each other out of <u>Der Untergang des Abendlandes</u> at some length while the <u>Black Destroyer</u> and the <u>Discord in Scarlet</u> crept closer and closer—but van Vogt soon abandoned this rather difficult thinker for the more manageable scholia of general semantics, Bates eye exercises, and scientology. My own "Okie" stories were also founded in Spengler (though I hope less obtrusively), which may be one reason why they reminded some reviewers of van Vogt. I can't think of a single additional instance.

the conventions of Magian physics (which Spengler c alls a "cavern" convention, a strikingly fruitful epithet in his hands).

Hence the customs, attitudes and fundamental assumptions of Earth are not only alien to the Ein worlds, but are becoming more so all the time, although only twenty years of Earth time (five centuries in the Ein system) have passed when the story begins. Note how carefully this relationship has been chosen: Were Ein time *slower* than Earth's, communication would have been impossible not only almost immediately, but also *in both directions*.

I shan't go into the plot, which is bewildering, and made more so by the fact that the three worlds of Ein are so completely alike—designedly—that it is hard for the reader to tell where he is from one chapter to another, though it's absolutely essential to the story to keep track of this. Given Lowndes' premises, I can think of no simple way this defect could have been remedied, except to suggest that the book might have benefitted by being longer—a prescription Lowndes could hardly have followed with this publisher even had he wanted to. As matters stand now, everything happens in a hell of a hurry, and a profusion of insights, ironies, comic strokes, plot turns, inventions, epigrams and paradoxes goes hurtling by before the reader has half a chance to savor them. An even greater penalty is that, in this enforced hurry to expose all the important facets of this complex notion—which would have occupied most other writers for twice the ten years Lowndes thought about it—the author's poetic gifts bubble briefly and then go down like a stone, leaving behind a prose which (except for its frequent wit) is no more than utilitarian. I can't very well blame Lowndes for this; but his book, like del Rey's (van Lhin's) *Police Your Planet,* is not in my judgment half the book it could have been if it could have been freed of Avalon's 45,000-word corset.

I recommend it, all the same. Unsatisfying though it is in some ways, it's packed to the eyebrows with ideas, and even its failures are unique.

WILLIAM ATHELING, JR.

And Another *October, 1961*

        If Robert A. Heinlein's *Stranger in a Strange Land* (Putnam's, 1961) is not the longest single science fiction novel of the last three decades, at least it has very few peers. Yet despite its length, it seems crowded, and for good reason: it is about everything. In the course of unfolding the plot—which is itself very rich in incident—Heinlein explores politics, aesthetics, ethics, morals, theology, the occult, history, economics, a double handful of sciences, and a whole hatful of subsidiary matters. The result is not only impossible to do justice to in a review, but almost impossible to describe or characterize; I hardly know where to begin.

In such circumstances it is the part of wisdom to follow the author's lead and begin at the beginning. The book is science fiction, as the opening sentence establishes firmly: "Once upon a time there was a Martian named Valentine Michael Smith." Smith is the bastard of an adultery which occurred on the first manned expedition to Mars, and the sole survivor. (It is quickly established that the book is not for children, also.) He has been raised from infancy by the Martians, and thinks of himself as one of them. He is the stranger of the title, and the Earth, to which he is brought back at about the age of twenty-five, is the strange land.

Ostensibly, the novel tells the story of his education, career, and fate on Earth, a standard gambit for a satirical novel with a long and distinguished lineage. Heinlein, however, does not follow the usual procedure of showing how ridiculous our Earth customs are to Smith's Martian eyes, except in very small part. This role is allotted to an Earthman, one more in Heinlein's huge gallery of marvellously crusty eccentrics, "Jubal E. Harshaw, LL.B., M.D., Sc.D., bon vivant, gourmet, sybarite, popular author extraordinary, and neo-pessimist philosopher," who takes Smith in when the heat becomes too great for the fledgling, and rapidly takes on the role of Smith's foster father. As a popular author, Jubal sits beside a swimming pool in the Poconos dictating amazingly soppy confessions, love stories, and anything else he can turn into money, to three beautiful secretaries who also help to run his household; as a "neo-pessimist philosopher," he is charged with interpreting everything on Earth to Smith, to

THE ISSUE AT HAND

everybody else in the plot, and to the reader. He is livelier as a philosopher, but much more expert at soppy copy; of this, more later.

As for Smith, he is often amazed at Earth customs but tends to be uncritical, largely because it is Martian to *grok* every experience (the word means to drink, to drink in, to understand, and a host of related concepts, like a Chinese root) in the hope of embracing it, rather than rejecting it. Thus he is enabled to accept many Earth customs for which Jubal has nothing but scorn, and sometimes seems to Jubal to be in danger of being swallowed up in one or another of them. And in fact one does swallow him; sex, which on Mars is completely sensationless, accidental, and uninteresting (but at which Smith proves expert "by first intention," as a surgeon might put it).

From this point on, *Stranger in a Strange Land* becomes so heated on this subject that it may well inspire twice as many would-be book-burners as Heinlein's *Starship Troopers* (Putnam, 1959) did.* Heinlein supplies no on-stage orgies, no anatomical details, and no washroom graffiti, nor does he ever adopt the pornographer's device of treating a woman solely as a sexual object; indeed, his attitude is about as far toward the opposite pole as it is possible to go, short of *Barchester Towers*. I choose my example carefully, for Heinlein's treatment of sex is confessedly, designedly, specifically reverent—and this very reverence has produced the most forthright and far-out treatment in the whole history of science fiction, guaranteed to turn bluenoses positively white.

At this point I am going to abandon the plot, which has already developed as many knots as a gill-net, and which in any event can be depended upon to take care of itself. It goes, as good Heinlein plots always do, and this is a good one. Now, however, I think I have reached a position from which to characterize the novel: It is religious.

No communicant to a currently established religion is likely to think it anything but blasphemous, but its dominant subject is religion, and its intellectual offerings and innovations are primarily religious too. The sex, the politics, the sciences, the action, all are essentially contributory; the religious material is central. The religion is a synthetic one, of which Smith is the

*It did; but also like its predecessor, it won the Hugo for its year.

Messiah (or perhaps only the prophet), and the main task of the novel is to show it as sane, desirable and exalting—in contrast to both the systems of large established orders such as Islam and traditional Christianity (toward all of which Heinlein is sympathetic and apparently well informed) and those of highly commercial enterprises like the California nut-cults (some features of which, with Smith's Martian assistance, he also manages to view with at least moderate tolerance).

Heinlein-Smith's eclectic religion is a fascinating potpourri, amazingly complicated to have come from a single brain rather than from centuries of accumulated haggling and hagiography; it contains something for everybody, or bravely gives that appearance, though by the same token it contains something repulsive for everybody too. I am not going to say which parts I like and which I don't, this being a purely private act of value-judgment which must be reserved by each individual reader to himself, but the solely intellectual parts of the structure are well worth some analysis, particularly since they are as often in conflict with each other as are those of all other Scriptures I have ever encountered.

Heinlein-Smith's system is pluralistic: it admits of no single God, but instead says *"Thou* art God"*; and if you are capable of understanding this sentence, then you *are* God whether you agree with the sentence or not. In other words, every being capable of thinking, understanding, embracing, is God, and that is all the God there is. Since a proper God cannot really die, survival after death is granted by the system (dead Martians continue to hang around the planet composing art-works and giving advice, but dead Earthlings go somewhere else, location not given); Heinlein shows directly (that is, without the intervention of Smith) that the dead are busy running the universe, as befits gods, and suggests in at least two places—though not explicitly—that they are at least occasionally reincarnated as "field agents." Because all who grok are God, there is no punishment in the hereafter; even the worst villain in this life graduates directly after death into being an assistant Archangel, though he may find himself not in a position to give orders to someone who was less villainous than he.*

---

*My flippancy of tone is not intended to denigrate the subject matter, but to reflect the treatment. Like George O. Smith, G. Harry Stine and other engineers-turned-writers, Heinlein sometimes tries to prove his characters wits and sophisticates by transcribing page after page

Thus far, then, the system resembles that of the "Perelandra" trilogy in its special emphasis on intelligence and empathy (you will remember that C. S. Lewis says that any *hnau* or reasoning being is a special child of God regardless of its shape or demesne); it also includes much of Schweitzer's "reverence for life," whether thinking or not, as is demonstrated early in the book when Smith is reluctant to walk on grass until he groks that it grows to be walked on; but there is no overall deity. The suggestion of reincarnation, if I am not misreading Heinlein in raising this question at all, is a common feature of Eastern religions, and I think it would naturally appeal to a writer trained in the sciences because it is conservative of souls, thus preventing the afterlife from becoming overcrowded beyond the limits of infinity and eternity. The implied dubiety about what really happens to the soul after death is Judaic, though without Judaism's 600-fold intellectual modesty on the subject; and the absence of any sort of punishment in the hereafter might be traced to many sects, a number of them Christian (see for example the heresy of Origen, who maintained that such was the mercy of God that if there is a Hell it must be empty).

Now, what are the implications of all this for the living? That is to say, how should we behave if all this should be true? Here the Heinlein-Smith religion, asked to supply its ethical imperatives, becomes a little murky, but at least a few doctrines can be fished up. Since there is no death—only "discorporation," a MaryBakerEddyism if ever I saw one—murder is not necessarily a crime. Under some circumstances it is wrong to push a soul on into the afterlife if it doesn't want to go yet, but if the adept "groks wrongness" (for instance, if the offender is threatening someone else's life and no easy alternatives present themselves) then he may kill without compunction. Smith frequently does this; he's the bloodsheddingest holy man since Mohamet, though he is delicate enough not to leave behind any actual bloodstains. The system implies that the true adept will always make the right decision in this matter; and besides, even if he's wrong he won't be punished. Not even the gas chamber can punish him,

---

of the painful traveling-salesman banter which passes back and forth over real drawing boards and spec sheets. There is not an intolerable amount of this in Stranger in a Strange Land, considering the length of the whole, but unfortunately the conversations of the dead in heaven are conducted entirely in this style. Though I value the Laughing Buddha for his laughter, I don't want him to sound like he is about to sell me a set of vacuum cleaner fixtures as soon as I'm suitably off guard.

since for the true adept discorporation can be no more than an inconvenient or inartistic exit.

In many other ways the system is ethically even more permissive, and it has no visible use at all for custom or morality. Because all experiences must be grokked to the fullest and embraced, and because the act of every grokking being is an act of a God, it would be very difficult to predict under what circumstances an adept would "grok wrongness," other than in circumstances where his own will or desire is about to be thwarted. Heinlein-Smith short-circuit this objection to some extent by making the sharing of experience (which equals the sharing of Godhead) superior to solo grokking. From this value-judgment emerges the novel's emphasis upon promiscuity, communal mating, orgy and voyeurism; there is an extended defense of the joys of strip-teasing and feelthy pictures which is both extremely funny (Heinlein's wit is surer here than it is almost anywhere else in the book) and rather touching (because it emerges from the completely unclouded naivete of Smith, who does not yet recognize, and indeed never wholly recognizes, how much heartbreak can be bound up even on the peripheries of sex). But the same value-judgment also allows Heinlein-Smith to read many people out of the Party as people it is not possible to grok with, and who therefore can be rejected and discorporated ("murdered" is a word *I* am fond of in this context) because they are boobs. (And besides, boob, "thou art God" and it doesn't really hurt.)

One of the more curious acceptances of the system is cannibalism. In part this emerges out of the givens of the plot: the Martians conserve food as they conserve water, and after an adult Martian discorporates, his friends eat him before he spoils, praising as they do so both his accomplishments and his flavor. This Martian custom is explicitly, if delicately, carried over into the Heinlein-Smith religion on Earth: In very nearly the last scene of the novel, Smith deliberately cuts off a finger, and his father-surrogate and his closest friend make soup of it. (It turns out to need a little seasoning; one suspects that so critical a remark would have been blasphemy on Mars, but the pun for once is pungent.) This scene has been prepared by a long analysis, by Jubal Harshaw, of the role ritual cannibalism has played in almost all the great Western and near-Western religions, in which the well-known present-day facts are buttressed at length

66

from Frazer.* Heinlein, also a thorough-going Freudian—as has been evident ever since "Gulf" (*Astounding,* Nov., Dec., 1949) —does not mean this equating of love, death, and high tea to pass unnoticed, but it is more interesting for its unorthodoxy than for its patness; Freud, a reductionist on the subject of religion, is here made to serve as the theorist for a ceremony of reverence. It's also interesting that in this scene the father eats the child, an act unsanctified in any society less primitive than that of guppies, and ruled out on Mars by the givens of Martian society; this is to my eyes the most extreme example of Heinlein's permissiveness, and he may have inserted it to suggest (as Smith himself has earlier suggested) that the Martianizing of Earth has gotten more than a little out of hand.

Almost all of the other ethical questions in the novel are subsumed under the head of bilking the mark, from the world of the carnival to the world of high politics—a subject on which Heinlein is as expert and amusing as always (and as infuriating to readers who believe that all grokkers are created equal). Their exploration takes up a substantial part of the novel, that part devoted mostly to Smith's education, but they pose few ethical problems unique to the system. Most of the crises are brought off by Jubal, not by Smith, without reference to the system, which is still in a state of very imperfect revelation while these machinations are going on. Most of the interesting minor characters, however, get in their licks in this earlier part of the book, and tend to fade back into the tapestry as the theology emerges— which is a shame, for they're a wonderful crew while they last. Thereafter, only Jubal and Smith continue to appear in the round. The others are ghostly and disconsolate, their promise not so much unfulfilled as pushed off onto a spur-line while the Powers and Propositions thunder by.

Nor does it seem to me that Jubal Harshaw's rather extended

*A minor puzzle is why the author has made Jubal so tentative on this point, especially in view of the enthusiastic way the novel tramples on toes considerably more sensitive. I do not see that it would have offended anybody—and it would have strengthened Jubal's case considerably—to have pointed out that in most major communions of the Christian faith, "Take My body and eat; take My blood and drink" is not only a symbolic command, but also and most explicitly a literal one, since the wafer and wine of the Eucharist not only represent but become the body and blood of Christ through the miracle of transsubstantiation (a point perfectly clear to every medieval Englishman through the much more vigorous, if more homely verb, "to housle"). However the character Jubal is speaking to presumably belongs to a Middle-Western Protestant sect which retains the ceremony but does not espouse transsubstantiation; a poor excuse, all the same, for dodging this point in favor of Frazer, whose doctrines are preached in no church whatsoever.

67

remarks on the arts constitute a true system of aesthetics referrable back to the central vision. Mostly, they are made in defense of representational or story-telling art, and this is what might be expected from a glorified, curmudgeonly and rich hackwriter, which is how Jubal is defined; so perhaps they are only characterization. The only other hint we are offered in this area is an account of a work of art which was being composed by a gifted Martian when he inattentively discorporated. Though Heinlein says that the nature (that is, the medium) of the art-work cannot be described, he makes it plain that this too is a story-telling work, and that the Martians are prepared to spend centuries thinking about its value. On this showing, if the Martians ever do turn out to be a menace we can ship them the score of Liszt's "Mazeppa" or a *Post* cover and immobilize them to the end of time. Heinlein-Jubal reads a fine story, instinct with the courage the author has admired and which is vaguely integrated into the religion of *Stranger in a Strange Land*, into Rodin's Fallen Caryatid, but except for a few such insights his aesthetics have always been those of an engineer and continue to be so here, neither contributing to nor detracting from his present subject.*

The final question I would like to raise—not the final one raised by the novel, not by a thousand—is that of the metaphysics of

*This raises once more the perennially interesting question of what Heinlein actually thinks, a form of mind-reading I would prefer to eschew if it were not that so much of this novel is specifically author-omniscent—that is, presented without the intervention of any character's point of view. The passage about the Martian work of art is one such; but again, it could be dismissed as only the groundwork for a plot point (though not a plot point of which the novel stands in any need, or of which any important use is made) rather than an illustration of the author's biases. This view would have the advantage of allowing Jubal's aesthetics to remain strictly Jubal's, and never mind that he is obviously the wise man of the novel--the only one who can grok without reading minds—whose opinions are more to be respected than anyone else's, even Smith's ninety per cent of the time.

It would also leave unposed the question of why, if story-telling is the essence of the best art, Heinlein is on record with an expression of contempt for opera. Under Jubal's aesthetics, the opera, the tone-poem and the song should be the supreme forms of music, while "absolute" music such as string quartets without accompanying literary programs should be as beneath notice as non-representational painting (presumably the work of composers who can't read music, as abstract painting is said to be the work of painters who can't draw). This is clearly one of the few questions about which Heinlein has not had the opportunity to think very much, and hence has formed convictions in the absence of data. He has never, for example, shown any interest in or knowledge of music. In Stranger in a Strange Land he invents a "Nine Planets Symphony" from which he can extract a "Mars movement" for a minor plot purpose, rather than invoking the famous work of Gustave Holst which, being real, would have served his purpose much better, and would have spared him the embarrassment of being caught with the notion that nine movements is a reasonable, let alone a likely number for a symphony.

The consequences for the novel in question are vanishingly small, of course; but it's interesting, if fruitless, to think of how much larger they might have been. Suppose that Jubal, during his tippy-toe discussion of the Eucharist, had happened to think of "Parsifal"?

Heinlein-Smith's system. Ordinarily this is a very late inquiry to bring to bear upon a religion, because it is usually accepted that God is only acting sensibly in not trying to make His early prophets explain quantum theory to a pack of goat-herders; better to stick to the ethical imperatives which the goat-herders should be able to understand with no difficulty, especially if the orders involved are accompanied by a rain of fire or some other practical use of physics. Later on, medieval scholars may presume that the God wrote two works, one being the universe conceived complete and perfect, and the other the Scriptures ditto; and still later, somebody (who will be burned for it) will ask why the metaphysics of the first work are so badly out of true with the metaphysics of the second. In the first or prophetic stage, however, this question is generally deemed unfair.

But it can hardly be deemed unfair to ask of a science fiction writer, who *starts* from assumptions about the nature of the real world which are as sophisticated as modern knowledge allows (this is not true of most of us, but it is true of Heinlein, at least by pure and consistent intention). In *Stranger in a Strange Land* he enforces the current acceptances of modern (scientific) metaphysics by beginning every major section with an author-omniscient review of how these events look in the eye$_{1961}$ of eternity; furthermore, he is scornful throughout of anybody (read, boobs) who does not accept this specific body of metaphysics.

So it is fair to ask him about the metaphysics of his proposed system; and it is, to say the best of it, a shambles. Smith appears on the scene able to work miracles, as is fitting for a prophet; in fact, he can work every major miracle, and most of the minor ones, which are currently orthodox in Campbellian science fiction. He can control his metabolism to the point where any outside observer would judge him dead; he can read minds; he is a telekinetic; he can throw objects (or people) permanently away into the fourth dimension by a pure effort of will, so easily that he uses the stunt often simply to undress; he practices astral projection as easily as he undressed, on one occasion leaving his body on the bottom of a swimming pool while he disposes of about thirty-five cops and almost as many heavily armored helicopters; he can heal his own wounds almost instantly; he can mentally analyze inanimate matter, well enough to know instantly that a corpse he has just encountered died by poisoning years ago; levitation, crepitation, intermittent claudication, you name it,

69

he's got it—and besides, he's awfully good in bed. My point is not that this catalogue is ridiculous—though it surely is—but that Heinlein the science fiction writer does not anywhere offer so much as a word of rational explanation for any one of these powers. They are all given, and that's that. Many of them, the story says, turn out to be communicable to Smith's disciples, but the teaching, unlike the love-making, never takes place on-stage and again is never grounded in so much as a square rod of rationale.

The more general features of the system fare equally badly. In what kind of continuum or metrical frame do the Martian Old Ones and the Earthly sub-Archangels live on—and in what sense do they live on? How is an intricate relational system like a personality conserved without a physical system to supply energy to it? What role in the vast energetics of the known universe can be played by the scurrying sub-managerial dead souls, and how are the pushes applied? What currently warrantable metaphysical system *requires* this illimitable ant-hill of ghosts; or, what possibly warrantable system *might* require it, and if so, how would you test the system? I think it more than likely that a brain as complicated as Heinlein's might have produced a highly provocative schema of metaphysics in support of the rest of the system; I don't propose these questions because I think them unanswerable, but only to call attention to the fact that Heinlein didn't even try.

Or perhaps he did, and the results got cut out of the manuscript. (Which was longer than the book; Heinlein did his own cutting.) If that is the case, had I been the author I would have cut the aesthetics instead, since they have nothing to do with the system; but I'm not the author, to the satisfaction of us both; so all that remains is that there's no accounting for tastes, as the master said as he kissed his Sears, Roebuck catalogue.* Certainly the version left us, for all its unknowable and/or visible omissions, is as provocative, difficult and outré a science fiction novel as Heinlein has ever given us. At the very least it will entertain you for months—or perhaps, if it does what it sets out to do, for the rest of your afterlife.

---

*Heinlein once remarked, in an autobiographical note, that he considered a Sears, Roebuck catalogue to be a greater cultural achievement than any opera.

Negative Judgments: Swashbungling, Series and Second-guessing

Autumn, 1953; Winter, 1953-54

THE NEGATIVE JUDGMENT, ONE OF our local gods said, is the peak of mentality. A good opportunity to breathe the air on that dizzy eminence appears in Poul Anderson's "The Immortal Game" (*The Magazine of Fantasy and Science Fiction,* February, 1954); that is, it is not a science fiction story, it is not The Chess Game Story the editors say it is, it does not have "incomparable romantic sweep" and it is not a "tragic epic." There are several more negative judgments one could apply, but let's stick for the moment to the value-judgments laid down for us by the blurb.

Boucher and McComas appear to have been goaded into this exhibition of editorial plank-walking by the dictum of Wilmar Shiras' character Timothy Paul: "In *Through the Looking Glass,* it wasn't a very good chess game, and you couldn't see the relation of the moves to the story" ("In Hiding," *Astounding,* November, 1948). This, let me remind you, is the dictum of a small boy described by Shiras as a budding superman; in this instance no evidence of supernormal intelligence is evident, however, since what he says of Carroll's joke is untrue.

If one is to set himself the task of writing a chess game story, the two desiderata laid down by Timothy are important—but even more important is that the story comes first. If the story is forced to follow the game to its detriment, even chess fans will prefer to take the game straight in the form of a chess problem —an option Carroll gives them—and people who want to read good fiction and do not have a passion for chess will also have been cheated. In addition, it would seem to me to be elementary to insist that the chess game involved be original with the writer. If he is to have the temerity to fool with the Master Game at all, it should become a part of the creative act, and be as carefully wrought to serve the needs of the story as any other set of background conditions would be.* The Carroll novel passes all of these tests, which is perhaps why it confuses small boys, Boucher and McComas, and (at a venture) Mr. Anderson.

Let's look at Anderson's story in this light. The game, first of all, is by admission not original with the author; it is instead a straitjacket imposed upon the plot from a textbook. The fiction as fiction consists in (a) a set of clumsy personifications of the chessmen, (b) a parenthetical passage attempting to explain the personifications by attributing them to "computers," and (c) a dollop of fan-fiction irony. It is child's play to follow the game through the story because there is no other plot but the pattern of moves, and the White and the Black sides and squares are differentiated by a system of name-keys cum typographical tricks which possess no advantages over the textbook practice of calling the elements of the game by their right names. Indeed, the whole purpose of the story's nomenclature is to help the reader translate it back into terms of the chessboard, thus leading him out of the story rather than into it.

Over this mechanical performance broods the spirit of Anderson the Barbarian, Thane of Minneapolis, Bard of Scandinavianism —the side of the writer's personality, in short, which emerged during his long apprenticeship to *Planet Stories*. Nobody should need to be reminded that Anderson can write well, but this is seldom evident while he is in his Scand avatar, when he seems invariably to be writing in his sleep. Boucher and McComas may see in all these romantic names and flourishes of battleaxes a "tragic epic" with "incomparable romantic sweep," but what the average reader is more likely to see is the style of a romanticist-manque, and he is more likely to compare it to Branch

*Hold on a minute, now. Why? Nobody faults Joyce for following the plot of the Odyssey, though many kick Updike for a similar use of myth; and allegory is an honorable form. Perhaps the difficulty is that all chess games are different, and as a class don't body forth a large enough set of common cultural assumptions to make any single game a useful underpinning for a story unless it's invented for the story on the spot. Anderson, in response to my original remarks, did indeed invoke allegory, calling the point he was trying to make "childishly obvious; but it seems to have escaped Mr. Atheling." Indeed it did, and does—I think, still, because the real, specific game between two real, specific masters confers far too high a degree of foreground specificity to support an allegory.

THE ISSUE AT HAND

Cabell than to Matthew Arnold.*

One of the surest signs of automatic writing is the duplicate or incantatory statement. "The Immortal Game" is full of them. Some examples:

> "Go, Carlon! Go to stop him!" (Cross at the green, not in between.)
> "Let me go, sire!" / "Let me go next."
> "To his death." / "They sent that fellow to his death."
> *Maybe we should have let Carlon die.* / *Maybe we should have let him die.*
> *Good! Oh, good, my Queen!*
> *He will retreat, he will retreat—*
> "Guard yourself!" / "Guard yourself, O Queen!"
> "Get free, Ocher!" she cried. "Get away!"

And so on. These are selected only from the speeches, both direct and indirect; the straight text is equally riddled with echolalia.●

This is in every way the wrong way to produce The Chess Game Story that we all would like to see. In my opinion, it has already been written by Lewis Carroll, but if Boucher and McComas are still searching (it is inconceivable that they can remain satisfied with this Anderson routine), I have a candidate of my own to offer. It is "Danish Gambit," by Carl Gentile.

"Danish Gambit" is a story based entirely in chess; it is ostensibly about nothing else. It is also a sociological science fiction story, the major premise of which cannot be deducted from the story (as it can from Anderson's) without ruining the piece. It personifies the chessmen, but in a way which leads the reader into the fictional situation rather than away from it. The emotional content of the story is not synthetic or derivative, but emerges directly from and bears upon human beings, not computers or stick figures—and from a situation charged with real

---

*I have no idea now why I chose these two names, unless it was because Boucher and McComas mentioned Arnold. Readers debating sword-and-sorcery fantasy tend to shed their heads as well as their shirts, as the recent Tolkien craze amply demonstrates. I might have made it A. Merritt vs. Homer to as little effect.

●Anderson invoked Hemingway in defense of this practice, but hindsight, it seems to me, can only make him uncomfortable in the example; even back then, Hemingway was becoming more and more to look like a textbook example of the shattered Thurber novelist who had discovered nothing but that everybody says everything twice. They always say everything twice.

73

terror, not from the needled mead of conventional battle-images. There is no single complete game in the story, but you won't miss it, since there *is* a story. And finally, "Danish Gambit" is written in the style of a man who had his full attention on his work.

Boucher and McComas almost surely have the story somewhere in their files, since it appeared in *Neurotica* #7 (Autumn, 1950)— the same issue of that little magazine which contained "Epizootics," G. Legman's crudely ferocious attack upon L. Ron Hubbard and Dianetics. They should reprint the Gentile story, I think, if only to take the taste of the Anderson out of the mouths of chess lovers and fiction readers alike; and primarily, of course, because "Danish Gambit" deserves the honor.*

Criticism in our universe of discourse crops up in curious places, largely because there is no traditional outlet for it as yet. One of the most delightful examples I've encountered thus far is a bit of verse-parody by Randall Garrett, called "I've Got a Little List" *(F&SF, November, 1953).* Though Garrett has had several● wooden, inconsequential stories published in the professional science fiction magazines over the past year or so— two of them so badly written as to require the assistance of a collaborator, Lou Tabakow, to raise them to the level of mediocrity —his verse can be read most profitably as the protest of a reader, rather than of a writer.

Echoing the executioner's aria from *The Mikado,* Garrett presents a list of science fiction writers "who take certain themes and run 'em in the ground." Sometimes in one line, and never in more than two, Garrett succeeds in striking off the characteristic preoccupations of most of the dedicated writers in the business, including many of the best of them—and doing it so well there can be no mistaking who he means, though he does not mention even a single name. The victims, in order, are Sturgeon, van Vogt, de Camp, George O. Smith, Dr. Winter, R. S. Richardson (when writing as "Philip Latham"), Hubbard, Blish, Asimov, the Kuttners, Leigh Brackett, Edmond Hamilton, Bradbury, and Boucher. (Incidentally, two of these attributions are questionable, but Winter and Hamilton both fit the specifications given by Garrett.) And the verse-maker says—and, I suspect, not entirely

*It still does.

●See page 31.

because he is copying W. S. Gilbert's verse form—that there are "at least a dozen others I could put upon the list...."

It would be easy for any of the authors thus pinpointed to observe that Mr. Garrett's list is not very highly selective. For one thing, it lumps series-stories with unconscious preoccupations: Hubbard and Sturgeon are pilloried (with some justice) for repeating themselves unintentionally, while Asimov and Blish make "the list" for writing series-stories for which there still seems to be some demand. Brackett is attacked for writing a cliche, space-opera (which she does), while Smith and Boucher are singled out for writing something which, however repetitious, is individual to each of them. Moreover, the list is wildly mixed as to the quality of the work associated with the authors named. The Kuttners, for instance, are master technicians, where Dr. Winter would not stand a chance against the author of the Bobbsey Twins. Hubbard is a sloppy writer, where Leigh Brackett is an almost glabrously smooth one. Sturgeon is an artist, as is Bradbury, where van Vogt and Smith are simply plot-happy writers with no special interest in or knowledge of English as a language. And so on.

All the same, "I've Got a Little List" is a funny verse, and one with bite. It is as effective as it is because it expresses a protest that we've all wanted to voice, at one time or another: the protest against the continual grinding of the same old axe, whatever the practical reason, or the unrealized reason. I've already raised my own complaint against Sturgeon's more and more intensive preoccupation with syzygy, and I was none too well satisfied with his answer (that his real subject-matter is all the forms of love); for one thing, his decision that he has only one thing to say as a writer will probably cripple him even more seriously than my initial stricture could have; so that I'm startled and discomfited to discover that Garrett...has spotted Sturgeon's preoccupation as a writer as specifically as I did, rather than in the general terms in which Ted himself chooses to describe it. That Garrett reads "synergy" for "syzygy" isn't too surprising; Garrett was once a chemist, and Ted's own use of the two terms is embarrassingly imprecise. The point: If a reader like Garrett can see that Ted is syzygy-happy, Ted might well stop worrying about defending himself from fellow writers, who are usually sympathetic as well as perceptive, and start asking himself why even the readers are beginning to think of him as a man with a crotchet. For a writer with Ted's gifts, such an inquiry would be worth-while, perhaps even life-saving; I doubt that it would do anything for some of the stumblebums and bummes listed elsewhere in Garrett's doggerel.

Garrett can, of course, do absolutely nothing for or about writers who are (1) too likely to bleed at the slightest harsh word to profit by any sort of criticism, or are (2) still being solicited by editors to carry on their series projects, even in the face of evidence that the readers have had enough, and even that the writers have had enough, too. The most recent Padgett "Baldy" story got written, after a lapse of years, because either the editors or the readership insisted that it be written, and in despite of the fact that Kuttner had told every friend in sight that he was stale on the series and didn't want to touch it again for an indefinite period. It turned out to be a good story, but it was also a tired one, as Kuttner had repeatedly warned that it would be. (I should add here that the Kuttners are not hypersensitive writers; few skilled technicians are. In support of my point No. 1 I could all too easily supply a list of easy bleeders, but I had better forbear.) As for the Okie stories, we know from Blish's own testimony that Campbell encouraged him to carry them on without limit; Blish himself said that he was ready to stop at a given point, but whether he will while his editors still remain tickled with the notion remains to be seen. (He didn't. Money talks.) As a writer he has plainly wound up the project—and none too soon for readers like Mr. Garrett.

I have said enough about Bradbury at this juncture to make it plain that I am not unqualifiedly admiring of his work, and that in some certain respects I think he has been bad for the field. I now find myself in the position of feeling required to defend him from one of his most passionate admirers—and not only Bradbury, but any writer of minimal competence.

Vide Kendell Foster Crossen's review (in *Future,* November, 1953) of *The Golden Apples of the Sun* (Doubleday, 1952). Immediately following a review by Damon Knight which praises Crossen as an acute critic, we find Crossen wishing upon Bradbury the services of some "creative editor," like Maxwell Perkins, the man who gave Thomas Wolfe's novels what small shape they possess. This is about equivalent to saying that Crossen loves Bradbury so much that he can wish him nothing better than an advanced case of smallpox. The fact of the matter is that for every writer like Wolfe who could be helped by a Perkins, there must be a thousand who wish that Perkins had been torpedoed in his crib. Wolfe was, by Perkins' own admission, one of the sloppiest writers who ever took to paper, and Perkins transformed him into a readable enough writer to make him an enthusiasm of Bradbury's and of some other people (mostly very young ones)—thus in one stroke encouraging other writers as lazy as Wolfe in the belief that decent story construction is the job of the editor rather than the writer, and at the same time encouraging every other editor to believe that he knows writing better than any possible writer.

(Editing in this country is usually the first job taken by a literary young man just out of college; and it pays so miserably that unless the young man makes a major find, like a Wolfe, which he can use as a carrot, he seldom lasts more than a year.)

One cannot now walk into an editorial office without flushing a sub-editor, or even a senior editor, who burns to be another Maxwell Perkins—in other words, to make his mark upon letters by showing some writer how to suck eggs. Actually, of course, not one editor in 600 knows enough about writing to justify his trying to explain, even to a beginning writer, anything more complicated than which end of a sentence is supposed to have a period on it—as the sorry record of editorial acceptances which I have been considering here makes most plain. The few exceptions are those editors who have previously proven themselves as writers, and even among these it isn't hard to find men who can't even begin to tell anyone else what might constitute a good story. But with Perkins as an example, thumpheads who have yet to discover English grammar have set themselves up as mentors and fathers to writers, including writers of long experience.

The science fiction field is no more overrun with these prickamice than is the rest of the book and magazine industry, but it's no less infested, either. Every time an established editor leaves a magazine and a previous underling ascends to the gold-plated potty, the former office boy gets the Perkins fever (one major symptom of which is a tendency to refer to Thomas Wolfe as "Tom"), and decides that every writer he deals with is going to have to relearn the craft in order to satisfy *him*. I once sat in on a comical luncheon during which one of these new godlings—

77

who had himself written a total of two published short stories, both of which stank in spades, both published by himself—spent two hours briefing a man with several hundred stories in print on the Basic Principles of Fiction while three other writers with similar histories attended with well-simulated awe.

Whatever you may think of Bradbury as a writer of *science* fiction, it's already plain that he is a superb technician, that he is also something of a poet, and that, above all, he almost always knows exactly what he's doing. If, in response to Crossen's gratuitous advertisement, some "creative editor" shows up on Bradbury's doorstep and offers to teach Bradbury how to write, I for one recommend that Bradbury spit in his eye.

And that should go for all of us. Criticism from fellow craftsmen is something none of us can safely do without—but a bas the creative editor. Damon, are you still convinced that a draftsman of your caliber has to regard Crossen's criticism as "acute"? If so, look out; he'll be calling for a "creative editor" for *you* next, and like as not you'll get one who talks about "Jim" Joyce, and recommends that you study comic-book balloons to improve your dialogue.*

The reappearance of Lewis Padgett in the September, 1953 *Astounding*—and with that Baldy story, at that—provides a fresh reminder for those of us who need it of how many worlds the Kuttners are away from the technical universe occupied by most of the new writers. "Humpty Dumpty" is not, to my eyes, the best Baldy story of the series, partly because it has its share of the symbols of resignation and defeat which have been creeping into the Kuttners' most recent writings,• but it is an object lesson in how to construct a science fiction novelette.

It manages to be so in spite of the fact that its basic construction follows a plan developed by the Kuttners a long time ago, and follows it rather mechanically at that. Padgett stories for years have begun in just this way: The narrative hook, almost always dealing with incipient violence, madness, or both; enough development of the hook to lead the story into a paradox; then a complete suspension of the story while the authors lecture the

---

*In reply, Crossen concluded that Atheling "seems to be slightly neurotic on the subject of editors (could it be that editors don't properly appreciate his talents?)"

•This tone, disturbing from so young and sane a man, had begun to creep into Henry's letters of that era as well. He died suddenly, early in 1958, at the age of 43.

reader on the background for a short time, seldom more than 1,000 words. The lecture technique is generally taboo for fiction, especially in the hands of new writers, and only two science fiction writers have managed to get away with it and make the reader like it, Heinlein being the other. "Humpty Dumpty" is no exception; it follows the pattern so predictably as to suggest that the Kuttners do not have their entire attention on their work.

And yet, automatic though some of the writing seems to be, the story is beautifully rounded as a structure, and, as is usual with the Kuttners, does not contain an unnecessary word. As a writing team the Kuttners evidently subscribe to Chekhov's principle of plot economy (the Russian writer once remarked that if in a story he mentioned that an ornamental gun hung on the wall of a room, that gun must go off before the story is over). For a single example, note the mention in "Humpty Dumpty" of the way Cody perceives the minds of the goldfish. Any other writer would have been so pleased with this as a bit of coloring matter —for, while it's logical enough that a telepath should be able to read the minds of animals, few other writers in the field would have conveyed the point in so bizarre a way—that he would have let it stand just as it was. Not so the Kuttners; that bit of color has to be for something, not just color for its own sake, and so toward the end of the story the goldfish are used as a springboard into understanding the mind of the child. This, gentlemen, is story-telling; and if more than half of Campbell's current stable could be forced to drink from the Kuttners' goldfish pond, *Astounding* would be a hell of a lot more readable than it is these days.

While I am in this unexpectedly mild mood, let me add a word about a newcomer who *doesn't* appear to need forcible technical instruction, but instead seems to be learning for himself, and at astounding speed. This is Algis Budrys, whom I nominate as The Man to Watch for 1954. Each successive story of his that I have seen has been better than, and quite different from, the preceding one; and each one has gone a little deeper into characterization, and has shown a surer understanding of story construction. Your special attention is invited to "Riya's Foundling" in the Columbia *Science Fiction Stories* (No. 1, 1953), for an example of what Budrys already can do as a student of the craft of plotting; and for a thoroughly convincing study of the retiring spaceship captain—superior by many miles to Lee

Correy's "And a Star to Steer Her By" (*Astounding,* June, 1953),
and in less than half the space—try "Little Joe," also in the
September, 1953 issue of *Astounding.*

One Completely Lousy Story, With Feetnote

Spring, 1954

SOME TIME BACK, DAMON KNIGHT wrote me a letter about this column in which he said, among other things, "...I think it's a waste of time to bring up your big guns against short-shorts by Charles E. Fritch. You ought to aim at the top, where the cliches are being perpetuated, not down among the black-beetles."

Perhaps so: I doubt that I can be accused of sparing the bigger reputations in the field, but I have several times torn newcomers to shreds, and will be at it again in just a moment. I think Damon has a different conception of what constitutes aiming "at the top" than I do, at least for the purposes of this column. I am not particularly interested in criticizing authors, known or unknown, in a vacuum. If there is to be any point in analyzing what is printed in the professional magazines, the analyses should also be read by editors, who are usually at least as guilty as writers when a nuisance is committed.

Furthermore, the excuse that editors cannot always get stories as good as they would like to print will not wash indefinitely. In particular, it cannot be used by an editor of long experience to justify the printing of a story which is not just a second-rate story, but a real stinker. When that happens, the writer's fault is secondary; he is ordinarily a beginner who hasn't had the experience to know just how thoroughly he has loused up his product. The editor should know.

To aim at the top, then, let's examine such a case of editorial collapse on the part of a great editor: John W. Campbell, Jr.

WILLIAM ATHELING, JR.

The story under consideration is "Final Exam," by a new writer (if that's the word I'm groping for) named Arthur Zirul. It appears in the March, 1954 *Astounding Science Fiction.*

The story is one of the worst stinkers ever to have been printed in the field. To begin on the most elementary level, Mr. Zirul's prose includes more downright bad grammar than any single *Astounding* piece since the George O. Smith yarns of the forties. Mr. Zirul's verbs and their subjects do not agree with each other in number ("no one outside of those present were even aware ..."); his sentences peter out into prepositions* ("Fastened to the belts were several instruments; none of which Honosura was familiar with ..."); and his punctuation is, to say the least, idiosyncratic (ibid.). Prepositional phrases dangle ("With a shout and a kick the animal clattered off, almost as frightened as its mistress ...") and so do subordinate clauses ("If nothing else, the relentless questioning had resulted in a limited vocabulary ...").

I shall not belabor this point, because almost everyone will agree, I think, that a reasonable command of the fine structure of one's language is the writer's first and most indispensable tool. If Campbell was bound to let Mr. Zirul's story by on its other merits (it has no others, as we shall see below), either he or Miss Tarrant should have made some attempt to turn it into English before it went to the printer. Or perhaps they did make such an attempt, and the bloopers which are still in the printed version of the story represent only a residue; after all, *Astounding's* proofreading has always been sloppy. If so, the thought of what the original grammar of the manuscript must have been like is horrifying.

Those of my readers who are none too sure of their own ability to manage grammar are by now curling their lips at that goddamn purist Atheling, and demanding to know what difference the grammar makes, after all, if it's a good story? Well, of course it makes a lot of difference, even to the best story in the world, for a writer who can't handle his own native tongue adequately instantly loses the confidence of his readers. In this instance—as is more usual—the bad grammar is used to tell a very bad story indeed; Mr. Zirul has committed so many other failures of technique that a whole course in fiction writing could

---

*So okay, Fowler sanctions this, to avoid constructions which would be clumsy and pedantic; but Mr. Zirul doesn't know the difference.

be erected above his hapless corpse.

His dialogue is terrible. All the speakers sound alike, and all of them sound like the narrative passages—that is, like Mr. Zirul himself. The text betrays an obvious reason for this failure. Mr. Zirul has concentrated upon *how* a thing is said, to the exclusion of *what* is said, which is exactly the wrong way to write dialogue. How do we know he's done this? An informal count of his speech-tags betrays it at once. About half of the 15,000 words of this story are dialogue, at a minimum estimate, and in the 7,500 words of miscellaneous yatter, the characters actually *say* something only twenty-seven times. For the rest of the yarn, they shout (six times), repeat, snap (twice), order (four times), stammer, observe (five times), ask (sixteen times), lecture, argue, "half-whisper," muse, call, sigh (four times), nod, agree (three times), report (three times), cry, yell, command, bark, scream (twice), guess, state (twice, both times "flatly"), add, suggest, chide, propose, announce, explain, exclaim, admit, growl, chuckle (twice), sneer, answer, mutter (twice), resume, gasp, bellow (twice), roar (twice), grunt, quote, fume, write (twice), continue and blare—a total of 89 more or less legitimate substitutes for "said," not counting about an equal number of illegitimate ones which we'll get to below.

Obviously, Mr. Zirul has in his possession a table or book of such substitutes, either compiled by himself or bought with good money, and he is using it to give his dialogue "variety." There are many reasons why this is a self-defeating project, of which three are important. For one thing, it is over-emphatic. Mr. Zirul has never met any group of people who used so many different tones of voice in conversation, and neither has anyone else. Such an assemblage of "said" substitutes cannot fail to make the story in which it is used sound to the ear like five minutes before feeding time in a bear pit. Secondly, it is redundant. All sixteen of the speeches tagged by Mr. Zirul with the word "asked" end with question-marks; that is sufficient. When a character repeats a word after another character, we do not need to be told that "he repeated"; we can see that. When a character says "N-No, sir," it is wasted ink to add, "he stammered."

Third, it inevitably leads even writers less tone-deaf than Mr. Zirul into morasses of approximation and bollixed construction. It is only a short step from the dubious "he half-whispered" to a

WILLIAM ATHELING, JR.

speech-tag like "he tinned," which is meaningless unless it is
soldering you are writing about. (How, I wonder, did Mr. Zirul
manage to leave out that favorite speech-tag of lady corn-huskers,
"he husked?") Then you abandon tags which represent sounds
(although these are the only legitimate reasons for using speech-
tags other than "said"—it is impossible, for instance, to suggest
in the speech itself that the character is whispering) and begin to
substitute facial expressions ("he smiled," "he beamed," "he
smirked," "he sneered"—what a procession into hysteria!) or
gestures ("he winced," "he shrugged"). Pretty soon you are
turning nouns ("he understated") or adjectives ("he flustered")
into verbs, and your gestures have left the realm of emotional
expression altogether ("he pointed"). The final step in this dismal
process—and Mr. Zirul takes them all, all the way out to the end
—is to start dropping entire sentences into the middle of your
speeches, sentences which have nothing at all to do with your
characters' manner of speaking, but instead only tell what *else*
they are doing while they are talking, and hence split their
speeches in two without taking any part in them. This results in
a text which reads, as Mr. Zirul's frequently does, like a fresh-
man translation from the German.

So much for the language in which the story is told; this
demonstration is, I think, detailed enough to indicate that neither
the writer nor the editor has discharged even a minimum responsibility to the readers. What about the structure of the story
itself?

There are two threads to the piece, neither one definite enough
to be called a "plot," and neither one connected to the other
except through the fact that about the same cast of characters
appears in both. Mr. Zirul gives us, first of all, a story about a
group of shipwrecked aliens who must get back together from
widely scattered landing points, and the difficulties involved in
making the rendezvous; once this is accomplished, there is tacked
onto it an aborted little effort to use the idea for another story,
in this instance the oldie about the aliens who unite us warring
Earthmen by faking an invasion. It takes Mr. Zirul nothing short
of forever to establish each of these two ideas—but it has never
even occurred to him that something ought to be done with ideas
after they have been exposed. Just getting the aliens' ship
wrecked and abandoned takes him about three thousand words,
not more than three of which were necessary, since story No. 1

84

cannot begin until after the aliens are on the Earth.

I keep insisting upon my assumption that such things have not occurred to Mr. Zirul because I want to emphasize the role the editor plays, or should have played, under such circumstances. Mr. Zirul is a beginner. He has had insufficient practice in the writing of fiction to have met more than a small fraction of the problems which are involved in writing a good story, and in addition he has not read enough of competent writers' work—or read it with enough understanding—to be aware of how competent writers tackle such problems. If he stumbles—and God knows he does—the stumbles don't represent flaws in his character, insufficient attention to his prayers, or outright malice or laziness on his part. They represent inexperience. The editor, who has had the experience, is the man responsible for Mr. Zirul's inexperience; that is to say, it is the editor's choice whether to inflict that inexperience upon the readers, or instead try to correct it before putting Mr. Zirul into print.

A conscientious editor, for instance, would have told Mr. Zirul that he had failed to make himself aware of so simple a technical problem in fiction-writing as that of how to handle the point of view. He would have pointed out that in "Final Exam" there is no consistent point of view; instead, the author is omniscient, and tells us what each and every character is thinking (including the horse). He would have explained that the author-omniscient method of handling this problem, while it is not necessarily always bad, is at the very least obsolescent, and that common practice in modern fiction is to assign a single point of view for a short story, or at the very most, a single point of view for each plot thread. This, the editor would explain, is not an arbitrary rule, but instead is based upon a great deal of accumulated experience as to how a reader reads, and what techniques give the reader the greatest access to what is important in the story. Modern readers in particular, the editor would be able to point out, are not used to being forced to leapfrog from one character's mind to another's at the author's whim; instead, they have been trained to identify with some single central character, and to be admitted to his thoughts only. Certainly no modern reader is going to react favorably to a point of view which may shift from one paragraph to another, or even from one sentence to another.

It would not have hurt the editor, either, to tell Mr. Zirul any of the other points mentioned above. They are none of them esoteric, and none of them arbitrary; they have come out of a body of common practice in fiction which Mr. Zirul is going to have to learn if he expects to make any headway as a writer. Certainly it can't be described as a favor to Mr. Zirul to put such a pre-adolescent effort as "Final Exam" into print, for the purchase of such a story implies general approval of the author's narrative techniques. Mr. Zirul is going to be baffled and hurt that his succeeding efforts are going to be bounced without comment by other editors in the field; he will think that Mr. Campbell's acceptance "proves" that his stuff is good, and "proves" the other editors wrong. Nobody, probably, will bother to explain to him that the purchase of "Final Exam" means nothing but that a once-great editor was asleep at the switch.

Of course, not everything that Campbell has published during the past year has been as incredibly inept as Mr. Zirul's story. Moreover, some of the magazine's flaws are of long standing: its proofreading, for instance. (If that sentence had been printed in *Astounding*, Miss Tarrant would have made the penultimate phrase read, "it's proofreading.") On the level of these minor flaws, such debacles as "Final Exam" indicate nothing more than the magnification of small weaknesses into policies—by which I mean that, where once we knew as a matter of course that *Astounding* was not very skillfully proofread, now we can hardly escape suspecting that it is not proofed at all any longer.

But beyond these minor quibbles, it now seems evident that there is no longer much editing—let alone proofreading—going on at *Astounding*.* The defection of most of Campbell's major writers to other markets has required him to develop a new stable, but to my astonishment, and I think to most other readers', he is slacking the job: he is emphasizing the new writers he favors by the simple statistical process of buying them more often, but otherwise he is offering them no guidance at all /beyond,

---

*Of course even bad editing remains a kind of editing, but inattention to the kinds of problems which traditionally concern editors is an unusually negative kind of bad editing. The stricture can still be applied today, despite much change in the physical shape and sumptuousness of the magazine. Throughout the intervening period, it has been clear that Campbell has been thinking of himself primarily as an educator, selecting stories for print primarily because they raise questions he wants to see put, make points with which he agrees, or otherwise act out his editorials in story form. Because his rates are relatively high he nevertheless finds some good work and seems genuinely glad to have it—but the sheer weight of pedagogy, much of it written as such on direct commission, has been overwhelming. Very recently there have been signs of reversion, though; let us cross our fingers, for no editor has ever matched Campbell when he had his mind on editing.

it must now be added, telling them *what* to say. There was a time when Campbell would have written Mr. Zirul a four-page letter, explaining to him what was wrong with his technique and how it could be bettered; now, Mr. Campbell prints Mr. Zirul, and that's that. If we turn to a much better new writer—Chad Oliver—we can see even more clearly where editorial responsibility has been relinquished.

Unlike Mr. Zirul, Mr. Oliver writes well and has something to say. He is certainly worth following; he isn't a major writer yet, by any means, but he could become one. If he is to become one, he could use some help. Probably his most obvious difficulty is overwriting (which puts him in a different class altogether from Mr. Zirul, who could hardly be said to be writing at all yet). Mr. Oliver has to be told by somebody—and it should have been Mr. Campbell—that you cannot put an emotional charge upon every event in a story, no matter how commonplace or how minor, without (a) depriving the really important events in the story of meaning, and (b) making the story at least twice as long as the material in it justifies.

There's a wonderfully bathetic moment in a recent Oliver *Astounding* story during which the hero, who is marooned on an alien world with a few companions, notices that night is falling. This event—which is a universal experience of men everywhere, and one which is so fully expected as to cause no comment or elicit any interest—is then made the subject of a brief emotional cadenza in the hero's thoughts; he is made to think: Yes, night falls, even here. Mr. Oliver seems to think that the fact of night-fall can be made to carry some form of nostalgia or homesick-ness, but the event is badly chosen. The hero might just as well have noticed, with equal surprise, that Yes, he had hair, even here, or that Yes, objects fell, even here. You cannot convert a universal commonplace into a carrier of emotion just by remark-ing on it. Campbell could have told Oliver that. Why didn't he? He's been publishing Oliver stories for over a year now, and every one of them has been too long and too consistently hyped-up, every one of them for this same reason. If Campbell wants to use Mr. Oliver as a key writer in his new stable, he is going to have to help Mr. Oliver get over this hump, or at least to make Mr. Oliver aware that it exists. Otherwise all that will come of it is a general consciousness that Campbell is publishing Mr. Oliver rather often, and a general bafflement as to why Mr.

WILLIAM ATHELING, JR.

Oliver doesn't become a more attractive writer with further acquaintance, and with further practice.

Scattershot *Winter, 1954-55*

So MUCH WATER (OR ETHER, IF WE were to believe Dirac in those days) passed under the bridge between my previous columns and the one which follows that it seemed hopeless to me to attempt covering all the magazine issues which had been skipped. As a general observation, however, I felt that conditions had picked up a little in my absence—which just might mean that I ought to have been absent more often; a horrible thought, but one which was to recur later. *Astounding* in particular seemed to me to look up in the last quarter of 1954, and *Galaxy* and *F&SF* at least got no worse. In January, 1955 then, these three journals looked like this:

Astounding Science Fiction

"The Darfsteller" by Walter M. Miller, Jr. This is an unexceptionable piece of work, providing that you do not share Damon Knight's view that its subject—the decline of the independent craftsman in the arts—is already old-hat. Anyone who has read the fiction printed in the literary quarterlies over the past decade could hardly help being fed to the teeth by now with such repeated keenings over the grave of handmade pottery, and probably the lament doesn't sound much fresher for being clad in the trappings of science fiction. Nevertheless, the trend is anything but over with; it is spilling over into industry now, with automation threatening to deprive human hands even of the stunning monotony of assembly line work; and the possibility of novel-writing, song-writing, sculpting and painting machines is becoming more and more distinct.*

I at least find Miller's play-acting machine and his displaced human actor highly convincing. The moral that he draws, furthermore, is refreshingly positive—as it would have to be for Campbell—and contrasts sharply with the snivelling tone of most writers on this subject. (Even Cyril Kornbluth, whose "With These Hands" in *Galaxy*, December, 1951 is in most respects his best story, could find no solution but suicide, though the futility of the act is disguised by a triumphantly sharp moment of insight and a burst of poetry.) Technically, the story is tightly constructed, told in a rather low narrative key to set off sharply individual dialogue. And for any of the many science fiction writers who once worked for a certain network television serial (*Captain Video*), there's a hair-raisingly accurate portrait of one of the show's (penultimate) Big Wheels.

"Field Expedient" by Chad Oliver. This long novelette does not actually begin until chapter three. The first two thousand words consist of a sort of culture portrait of Earth in the year 2050, which uses a learned-sounding anthropological drone to establish nothing more than the familiar picture of a static civilization. Oliver himself sums it up in four words—"Don't rock the boat"—and needed no more. Once the leading characters are on Venus, the story picks up somewhat, and the anthropological material is used to create several interesting imaginary (and synthetic) tribal cultures, to be tied together in due course into an overall civilization which has been conditioned to respect diversity. The question of whether or not this plan is going to succeed provides the only suspense the story has (despite a desperate and wholly unsuccessful attempt to liven it up by keeping the Big Boss' *real* motive a mystery; the answer is utterly bathetic). In short, Oliver's decided talent is still being smothered by his over-writing.

"Armistice" by K. Houston Brunner is the only short in the issue worth noting here. The story it has to tell is far from exciting or even unusual, but the writer has a Vance-like eye for

*Painting machines are now common arcade and sideshow attractions.

sensuous detail which I found persuasive.

Galaxy Science Fiction

"The Tunnel Under the World" by Frederik Pohl continues the writer's feud with advertising into an improbable but circumstantially-told mechanical nightmare. Competent though the story is, it is spoiled for me by the excesses Pohl commits in giving samples of the ads used by the villains. The examples offered by Pohl and Kornbluth, both together and separately, in other stories have been revolting enough but remained funny because of their visible relationship to what is being committed today. "Cheap freezers ruin your food. You'll get sick and throw up. You'll get sick and die.... Do you want to eat rotten, stinking food? Or do you want to wise up and buy a Feckle, Feckle, Feckle—" is no longer satire, however. It is the naked hatred of the author, screamed out at the top of his voice.

"When You're Smiling" by Theodore Sturgeon is a hate-piece, too, but it is never out of the author's control for so long as three words. Ted's portrait of the man who enjoys causing pain is that of a man who thoroughly deserves the author's loathing. But by taking the pains to tell the story from that man's point of view, and to convey some of the man's enthusiasm for himself and his researches, Ted has made sure that his evil character does not emerge as an unbelievable caricature. The deeply subjective approach unfolds on the page with an air of pure objectivity, as though the author were simply presenting the character as he is, with an invitation to the reader to pass his own judgment; the author is loading the dice, to be sure, but entirely below the level of the reader's attention.

"Squirrel Cage" by Robert Sheckley is another of the interminable AAA Ace series, this time so awful as to read like a crude burlesque of all the others. Why should a man who wants his farm decontaminated deliberately withhold crucial information about the nature of the infestation from the firm he's hired to do the exterminating? Why does this exact thing happen in all the AAA Ace stories? Why don't the partners of AAA Ace wise up?

91

As usual, the problem is "solved" by pulling three rabbits out of the author's hat (though of course he doesn't call them rabbits— they *look* like rabbits, but if you call them smeerps, that makes it science fiction). It is nothing short of heart-breaking to see a once-promising writer settled down into the production of such pure trash. Sheckley's work has been getting lazier and lazier since the slick magazines took him up, but I think few of us expected to see him hitting rock bottom as soon as this. /To his credit, he bounced, though it took a long time./

"Perfect Control" by Richard Stockham is almost as bad. If there is anyone in the room who believed in the "great inventions" made by the characters in this yarn, he should stay away from Fred Pohl's commercials, or he will wind up owning all the Feckle Freezers in existence.

Finally, let me record my dissent to the proposition, voiced by H. L. Gold on the last page of this issue, that Evelyn E. Smith is "becoming one of the top writers of science fiction." If "The Vilbar Party" is a typical Smith production—and thus far it is— she is fast becoming one of the most prolific writers of "call the rabbit a smeerp" copy, and that is all. In this instance, a "cocktail" gets changed into a "vilbar." As for science content, the leading character is a Saturnian who spends a long time on Earth without any physical protection. How does Miss Smith explain this? She doesn't.

The Magazine of Fantasy and Science Fiction

"Selection" by J. T. McIntosh raises the point that all the planets, bar none, may be almost intolerable to live upon. It also denies the possibility—by ignoring it—that at least in some cases somebody might get at the causes of incompatibilities and eliminate them. This quality of radical incompleteness—of failure to think a proposition through to even its most obvious first derivative—is characteristic of this author, and I find it distracting. No matter how well a story may be handled in other respects, I cannot rid myself of the feeling that it has a large, jagged hole in it—a hole for which there is no excuse. What McIntosh has to say here about the adaptability of people in extreme situations was well worth saying, and I applaud it; but it is deprived of most of its force by my consciousness that the author's "inevitable" situation could remain inevitable to his characters only if they are assumed to wear horse-blinders throughout the story.

"One Ordinary Day, With Peanuts," is a Shirley Jackson story; that is all that needs to be said for it. Like John Collier, she is an original and a specialized fantasy writer, a born story-teller, and limited in her appeal. I love the stuff.

"Single Combat" by Robert Abernathy offers a character sketch of the man who will plant The Bomb in the middle of The City, and does a howling good job of it. It is neither science fiction nor fantasy, but it's skillfully handled in such a way that you may consider it either—or both—if you like.

Pauline Clarke's "The Potato Cake" retells the story of the Judgment of Paris in a thick Irish brogue. I cannot imagine why. "The Girl in the Ice" by Emyr Humphreys is a reprint from the British weekly *New Statesman and Nation,* which I remember having read in that paper. It is as quietly horrifying as ever.

"The Expert" by Mack Reynolds is a prime example of the incestuous science fiction story—that is, a yarn which depends for its effect on overt cross-references to science fiction itself. Anthony Boucher is addicted to this kind of story—as a matter of fact, he has written several*—but I can think of very few trends more dangerous to the field both artistically and financially. An increase in the percentage of yarns of this kind would be the quickest imaginable way of turning science fiction into a closed circle of mutual appreciators, speaking a jargon comprehensible only to themselves, and fatuously satisfied to have it that way. In short, a form of fandom.•

There are also two detective stories in this issue, one by John Dickson Carr, the other by Isaac Asimov. The Asimov is described as the first of a series, but it is already petrified and dead—a plain case of trying to graft part of a rigid corpse onto a living idiom. The other fiction item in this issue, "The Shop-

*"Not several—just one," Tony replied in an injured tone. He was correct. It just seemed like several.

•Another danger in this approach is that it courts laziness. Witness Fritz Leiber's 1964 novel The Wanderer (Ballantine), in which Leiber "explains" his gimmicks and assumptions by referring the reader to other science fiction stories.

dropper," is by a man who believes that the invention of names like Schnappenhocker is a hilarious pastime. Tiptoe by him quietly; he probably picked up the idea, poor fellow, in Gavagan's Bar (the locale of a series of stories that appeared in *F&SF* and *Weird Tales,* by L. Sprague de Camp and Fletcher Pratt, which managed to exhibit both these huge talents at their lowest common demonimeter. The *Tales from Gavagan's Bar* were gathered under hard-covers by Twayne Publishers in 1953).

One Way Trip *January, 1962*

Is ANYBODY READING? IF THERE IS
any question which distresses me about science fiction, it is this
one. It distresses me because I can't think of any way to get an
answer, not any more.

Writers shouldn't inflict their problems on readers, who presumably have more important things to think about; but if the
writer *has* no readers, he has lost his reason for living, no
matter how much money he may be making by running a type-
writer. And I for one no longer know whether or not anybody is
reading the stuff, and in this I am not alone.

Consider: What an editor buys reflects what he likes to read,
and what he thinks will sell. Six or eight months later, he may
find out that Vol. XII, No. 9 of his magazine sold very badly, but
he has no way of telling which of the eight stories in that issue
depressed the sales. If it sells very well, he has the inverse
problem. The usual out is to blame the failures on the readers
and the authors, and claim the successes for the editor. This is
human and I point no fingers; but it's no help to the writer.

There was once a time when the editors of science fiction
received letters from their readers—a very rare situation elsewhere in specialized fiction, and one that the editors of the day
were quick to use to their profit and to that of their writers.
They used these letters in three ways: (1) They spot-checked
what was unpopular with the readers, whether it be technical
inaccuracy, too much mushy love stuff, over-emphasis upon
atomic doom or some other crotchet, or a simple preference for

Author A over Author B; (2) They passed what they learned on to the authors, as well as re-balancing their issues from the new knowledge; and, (3) They printed many of the letters, thus providing a feedback mechanism through which the readers could learn whether or not they agreed with each other, and whether or not they were developing crotchets of their own (as of course they often were, being even more human than editors). It also happened that editors used letters from readers to prove themselves right, and to puff their magazines; but if you will look back at the letter columns of science fiction magazines when there *were* such columns, you'll find remarkably little of such puffery compared to the amount of genuine criticism and argument that was then being printed.

This situation no longer exists. Dignity set in—and in this instance I think "set in," as in a disease, is the right phrase. The editors, most of them, concluded that a magazine without a letter column is more dignified than a magazine with one. Though the excuses given for dropping the letters were very various, it is noteworthy that the columns were all dropped at about the same time that the magazines were going in for abstract illustrations in two colors, scholarly blurbs, big-name mainstream writers, and other symptoms of status-seeking. One of the most remarkable excuses ever offered for this policy was that the readers themselves had voted to drop the letter column (as could easily be proved by the letters received, the editor said, were there any way to get a look at them). And the most influential magazine to retain its letter column had long ago converted it into a discussion forum for the editor's crotchets, thus shutting out almost all feedback on the fiction in the book. (This danger had always been hovering; "letter comments"—meaning the editor's practice of having the last word in a letter column— have been with us from the beginning /and readers have always been divided about the ethics or even the simple desirability of the practice/.) But now most printed letters, and there are damn few of them, don't get into the book unless they are editorial comments, i.e., arguments picked with some previous position taken by the editor. (Of course he still gets the last word; the difference is that he has now worked out a way to have the first word, too.)

Under these circumstances it should hardly be surprising that science fiction readers stopped writing letters to magazines, except for those few readers who shared the editor's crotchets or wanted to argue with them. Feedback between author and reader disappeared, so far as the stories were concerned.

Readers' preference tallies? Well, they were a noble effort. They are, essentially, popularity contests; readers are urged to vote for the best story in a given issue; the story that gets the most votes wins the author a bonus, and so does the story that winds up in second place. I have received several such checks (which I drank), so I have no special reason to complain about the system. But it is plainly a fraud..../From here on for several hundred words, my original piece discussed the mathematical vulnerabilities of the "AnLab" system, including the several ways in which it can be and has been faked, but I see now that these criticisms, while valid enough, are beside my point: that AnLabs may tell an author that his story placed first, or last, but nothing about *why*. To this point, only my final anecdote was pertinent/: I know one writer who used all his relatives and friends to load up the voting, too, although in his case there was no possibility of a bonus—the magazine involved didn't give one. He seldom failed to rate high—but what for? The writer who wants to know what his readers think should be happier to lose this kind of contest than to win it.

The last remaining professional source of feedback for the science fiction author is the book review, and here the situation has gone beyond the worthless into the scandalous. Reviews of science fiction books no longer appear, except by accident, in the major review organs, such as the Sunday book sections of the New York *Times* and *Herald Tribune.* They do not appear *even* by accident anywhere else (in the United States—v. my DisCon speech, "An Answer of Sorts," below), except in the science fiction magazines themselves.

And the science fiction magazines, the last (and, a naive man might think, the first) point of contact between science fiction writer and science fiction reader, currently conduct their review columns almost solely on the assumption that anything that appears outside the magazine is a potential competitor and must be put down. (*F&SF* in particular for some time forbade its reviewers to notice any paperback books that were not reprints from *F&SF*—a policy which lost them the services of the inventor of serious science fiction criticism, Damon Knight.) The majority don't review books at all, although they manage to find space for fillers about virtually every other imaginable subject, from saucers to half-page puns called Feghoots. Those who still retain book reviews fill up the small space they allot to them with typographical tricks, with the crotchets of the reviewer (I refer only to crotchets which have nothing to do with fiction, such as saucerismo, bulletins about conventions, and personal anecdotes), and with reviews of science-fact popularizations which the reviewer, nine times out of ten, is utterly incompetent to assess. The science fiction book which manages to squeeze in among all these paragraphs of miscellaneous yatter is, by a natural law known as reviewer's obsolescense, so long out of print that no reader could find it even if he wanted to.

The financial harm which is done to the author by this situation is perhaps arguable, though I think it real. What the author does inarguably lose is technical criticism, far and away the most valuable kind, no matter where he finds it. He used to find it in the letter columns—and he paid close attention, if he had any sense at all. In the brief heyday of close book reviewing in the magazines, he got it from his fellow authors, too, for many of them took to technical criticism with great zest, and, usually, to good purpose. But if he looks at the book reviews in today's science fiction magazines, he finds most of the space devoted to "A Child's Guide to Molecules" or other such laymen's books on what purports to be science, reviewed by a man who ordinarily cannot count up to two without going down the hall to borrow the Monroe calculator from the sales manager—and often written by one, too, for good science popularizers are still rare.

I can't speak for anyone but myself, but I would consider that I had lost my mind were I to buy a science-fact book because a review in a science fiction magazine said I should. "Science-fact" in our field has become a synonym for fraud and saucerism, but even before this happened, I knew better sources for authoritative reviews of scientific books; for example, *Scientific American,* or the now-extinct *American Scientist.* Can anyone suggest to me any circumstances under which I would be justified in reading, let alone trusting, a review of a book about stellar evolution by the ex-brother-in-law of a science fiction magazine editor? (This situation no longer prevails, but it existed at *Galaxy* for years.) Or, to put the best possible face on the matter, though I have good reasons to listen attentively when Alfred Bester talks about protozoology or descriptive astronomy, Fred Pohl about

98

the theory of sets or P. Schuyler Miller about archaeology, why should I be patient with them when they do this in the book review section of a science fiction magazine? Why, I beg to ask, are they not talking about science fiction, in the very little space in which they are allowed to do so? None of these men are authorities on the subjects I have associated with them, and if they were, they would be talking about them somewhere else; they are amateurs, expressing amateur opinions, lovable perhaps but hardly reliable; any man who believes that a science fiction writer (or editor) is a reliable reviewer of scientific texts, or popular histories of the sciences, is a logical target for any form of quackery and deserves no better than he gets.*

In the meantime the reader of science fiction is ill served, and the writer starves—not for money, there is no particular shortage of that, but for contact with the reader. What is left behind —and it is valuable—is fan mail, and the fan press, upon which the writer who cares whether or not he is being read is now almost wholly dependent. This means that he is learning more about his writing from fewer and fewer readers. Even though he may have several paperbacks in print which have sold in the hundred thousands, his fan mail audience is inarticulate ("I liked your Foundation stories, when are you going to write another?") except for the crackpots who accuse him of stepping on their toes; out of a readership (or at least, a sales record) of better than five million, accumulated over 22 years, I have only 56 letters from book readers, and 47 of them were written to tell me that I was a dirty fascist, Jesuit, nigger-lover, liberal, Communist, Madison-Avenue brain-washer, anti-Semite, corrupt capitalist apologist, bisexual pervert, aesthete or propagandist for XXXism (supply your own term here). Though I can't deny one or two of these accusations—if I did, it would cost me money —what impresses me is that letters written directly from reader to author are rare to begin with, and secondly seldom have anything to say about the story; they are written to pick fights, usually regardless of whether or not the story was a good one. Quite frequently, the writers are so incensed that they ask the publisher not to buy from the author any more, though the letter-writer has spent only 35¢ for the writer compared to the publisher's $2,500; sometimes, indeed, they ask for their money

---

*I have twice reviewed serious texts—not popularizations—on relativity for science fiction magazines, and hence am my own most absurd example here.

back. (And they get it.) But in the world of ideas, two-and-one-half crackpot letters per year is no guidance at all (I got the biggest batch of hate mail in response to a marginally anti-McCarthy novel, about which I was then certain, and remain certain, that I was right and the letter-writers dead wrong), and it would be no help to me were those two-and-a-half letters instinct with the wisdom of the ages.

"What thou lovest well remains; the rest is dross." Science fiction is a small field and sometimes a funny one, but after two decades I can hardly pretend that I don't love it; and I'm distressed to find that, no matter where I publish what I write, I can't find out what other people think of it, in any way that I can trust.

But a return to the widespread *fiction* reviews of the early fifties, and a wholesale revival of magazine letter columns, would please me inordinately, and possibly make me write better. What is more to the point: it might make most science fiction writers write better. As of this moment, we do not know what the reader thinks—as he has been complaining for years—and even worse, we have no way of finding out.

The Short Novel:
Three Ranging Shots and Two Duds
July, 1962

THE JUNE, 1962 *ANALOG* LEADS OFF
with "The Weather Man," a "short novel" (32 pp.) by Theodore
L. Thomas which repays close reading. Thomas' work has been
appearing regularly in the field recently, and until now it had
struck me as being all of a piece: workmanlike, serious, only
moderately ingenious, and somewhat wooden. "The Weather
Man" might have been written by a different author; it suggests
with surprising suddenness that Thomas may very well wind up
a front runner in our field.

Like the rest of his work, it is serious in both content and
approach, but the resemblance to previous Thomas ends there.
As a piece of construction, it is not workmanlike in any ordinary
sense, though much labor has gone into its fashioning. The story
deals with an attempt by the tripartite Weather Council, an
international body with the muscles but not the name of a world
government, to produce snow over one square mile of southern
California in mid-July. This is patently a slight notion which
might have been thought up at the last minute to make a short-
short story to fill a hole in a fan magazine, but in Thomas' hands
it is made to yield all sorts of dividends, thanks in part to the
unconventional structure he has adopted.

The story has no hero nor even any central figure, despite its
title, which has been chosen to emphasize a crucial ambiguity.
Thomas begins with a powerful Weather Councilman, who
maneuvers the Council into granting the apparently crackpot
request from Holtsville, Calif., to help advance his own political

career. At this point the story leaves the Councilman permanently and introduces us to a woman mathematician of the Weather Advisors, upon whom devolves the job of figuring out just how the desired snow might be produced; her career, too, is at stake. Next we meet a captain of a "sessile boat" (a most curious name, for "sessile" means "attached to the substrate by a stalk," which the boats are not; but Thomas has good reasons for that, as for even tinier details), one of a fleet which cruises the Sun's atmosphere to make the weather demanded by the Council and calculated by the Advisors; his career, too, is at stake, to say nothing of his life and the lives of his crewmen. Finally, the snow falls... on an old man in Holtsville who just may have been the inventor of the sessile boats, although the credit has gone to someone else. (The healing power of exactly this symbol was engraved into English literature—for all time, I suspect—by Joyce in "The Dead," but one of the lesser miracles of "The Weather Man" is that Thomas arrived at this solution *both* independently *and* in the face of a previously expressed impatience with symbolism as a fictional tool.)

No one of these people is *the* weather man, unless Ted intended to hint that the dying Andrews is; but together, they all are. The weather that is produced is a complex, dependent upon all their skills, and in addition is a product of their special interests, including their personal interests and peculiarities. Except for Andrews, they are given vivid portraits, in far more subtle colors than Thomas has ever attempted before. This is all the more remarkable when you consider that they are thoroughly conventional figures: the Big-Shot Politician, the Brilliant Scientist, and the Heroic Spaceship Captain. Of the three, the scientist is the oddest and therefore the most interesting, but all three are real and alive. The three milieus are also well done, but here the honors go to the scenes on the Sun, where Ted gives us a piece of "hard" science fiction a la Hal Clement, a spectacularly ingenious (and radical) idea, a liberal helping of bright and unfamiliar colors, and a whale of an adventure, brief though it necessarily is.

There are obvious drawbacks to an experiment of this kind. The lack of a central character gives the reader nobody with whom he can consistently identify himself. The three major shifts of milieus mean that the reader must meet, and become able to identify, a completely different *set* of characters every ten pages. In no instance are we told the outcome of the ambitions of the three major figures—that is left to implication, as is the question of the validity of Andrews' retrospective claim to fame. An author who sets himself so many technical problems in one story must know in advance that they *are* problems before he can work out ways to surmount them; an achievement of this order can't be pulled off by luck or inspiration.

The inspiration is there—it is responsible, I should judge, for the imaginative sweep imparted to what at first glance seems a most unpromising notion; for the solid, yet vibrant characterizations; for the evocative quality of the Sun section, and of the immobile, dying, barely-seen man in Holtsville on whom the last snow is impossibly falling—but what makes it go is craftsmanship. I can only wish that the story had been longer.

Hooray.

Lest anybody begin wondering whatever happened to Atheling the Sourball (as his tribe affectionately called him), let's turn at once to "The Sound of Silence," by Barbara Constant, in the same issue. Miss Constant may be a perfectly real writer operating under her own perfectly real name, but this sample of her work reads like Judith Merril deprived of her underline key. It's all there: the repetitiousness, the chintzy little middle-class femininities ("She moved listlessly, showering, patting herself dry, lingering over the choice of a dress until her mother called her from the kitchen"...."counted the number of pleats in the billowing drapes"...), the preoccupation with sentimentalized small children, the parenthetical internal monologues, the feminine over-emphasis ("'I don't LIKE having you sit where I can't see you,' she said crossly."..."'I'm not a...a mutation. I'm not, I'm not, I'm NOT, and you can't say I am, because I won't listen.'"), and the inaccurately visualized glamour background ("In...certain industries—especially advertising— —'I have an appointment with my psychiatrist' was a perfectly acceptable excuse for leaving work early.").

The heroine is young and rich—though Miss Constant does not put the matter quite that lucidly. Indeed, what she says is that the heroine, whose name is Lucilla, "had been born twenty-two years earlier in undisputed possession of a sizable silver spoon." (It takes a long time, at 3¢ a word, to get anything said if you insist upon saying it like that.) She is bright, beautiful, in per-

WILLIAM ATHELING, JR.

fect health, and adored by her family and friends. Miss Constant
tells us that she is also charming; for instance, she responds to
a proposal of marriage with this engaging witticism: "Thanks,
but no thanks."

The lady's Trouble, as if you hadn't guessed it already, is that
she is telepathic, and hence can't marry the man she loves, who
is just a clod. At this point, gorge rising, I will tiptoe out of the
psychiatrist's office ("'It's unpolite to innerupt, Daddy'") and let
you finish the story yourself. Of course you can't sell it to
Analog again, but *F&SF* ought to be good for about nine more
versions of it.

A gifted, well-to-do girl whose Trouble is that she is telepathic
is also the heroine of James H. Schmitz' "Novice," the second
major offering in the June *Analog*. (It is four pages shorter than
the "short novel," so it gets billed as a novelette.) But what a
difference! Schmitz' heroine is an adolescent, who has for a pet
an alien creature called a crest cat with which, under special
circumstances, she is in difficult mental communion. The cat—
one of the most vivid and charming aliens anybody has invented
in years—is a zoo escapee of what is actually the dominant
species of its planet, but is unaware of this until the girl brings
it to that same planet on an engineered vacation—engineered by
an aunt who means to deprive the girl of her pet as part of an
elaborate act of indirect revenge. How the heroine and the cats
go about circumventing this, and incidentally winning for the cats
recognition as a civilized species, is the substance of the story,
which is told with Schmitz' usual elan, sense of color, and feeling for drama—as well as his muted, delicate instinct for the
comic. The story proves, if such a thing needed proving at this
late date, that telepathy can be a highly rewarding theme in the
hands of such fresh and hardy perennials as Schmitz and Jack
Vance, who seem to take it seriously and hence almost never
even bother to gum over the soggy cliches of the subject. I don't
myself think that there is any such thing, and I am as weary as
anyone could be of *Analog's* assumption of divine mission to
spread its gospel: but it was salutary of Schmitz to remind us
that it can, after all, be a delight.

Our anagrammatical acquaintance Darrel T. Langart's* two-

*Randall Garrett.

part serial, "Anything You Can Do!" (exclamation point optional), concludes in this issue. It tells us how a fearsome alien landed on the Earth and created a reign of terror, so that the Earth had to create a superman to cope with it. Earth's authorities have known the location of the Nipe's hideout for years, and have also figured out just how it thinks—an analysis which turns out to be entirely without faults, even minor ones. The hero's only job is to sneak up on the Nipe and, with the aid of superior reflexes, knock the creature down in a duel of fisticuffs as formal, and as unlikely, as those depicted in the boxing manuals of John L. Sullivan's day (and appropriately illustrated in the magazine in just that style). There is also some psionic jazz about the hero's developing identity with a handicapped twin brother, which has something to do with the main story, but not much. The total effect is at once mechanical and disorganized—a difficult compound to achieve, I agree, but why bother?

The August, 1962 *Galaxy's* definition of a "complete short novel," Jack Vance's "The Dragon Masters," runs to 87 pages, a nice fat parcel of words compared to *Analog's* dollop, even though *Galaxy's* body type is two points larger.

The story itself is wild and wonderful, if you like swashbuckling written by a magician—and I do. Like much Vance copy, "The Dragon Masters" is a fantasy of the far future, in which technology has receded so far as to make blade weapons, armor and animal mounts practicable once more, and in which an important place in the plot for magic (not just the belief in it, but its effective use) seems natural.

Poul Anderson has used this kind of atmosphere and approach several times to produce a mixture—part poetry, part comic effects produced by the juxtaposition of magical gestures with grittily rational explanations of why they work the way they do— but the overall tone ultimately is reasonable, not magical. L. Sprague de Camp has done this even more often; but in Sprague's comedies, the explanations of the magic are so determinedly those of an engineer that one suspects some of the comic effects of being unintentional; Sprague often seems to be debunking magic, whereas Poul is well aware that "explanations" derived from current theoretical physics are at least as mystical as anything one could find in a grimoire. To cite a single pair of examples: where Sprague predicates the behavior of a magical

WILLIAM ATHELING, JR.

sword in a battle upon the known tensile strength of the metal he
has said the sword is made of, Poul explains the traditional un-
luckiness of stolen fairy gold with a nuclear transformation which
is not only ingenious but radically inappropriate to a fairy-tale
atmosphere.

Vance's time-remote fantasies seem indifferent to the whole
problem, let alone its various possible solutions. They happen
in a timeless medieval world where questions of technology are
at best only excuses, and as likely to be based in magic as in any
other theory or ritual. This is reflected in his technological
vocabulary, which is thoroughly freighted with medieval terms—
wambles, potions, elixirs, popinjays, fuglemen, cornets, knights,
and of course many clangorous details of thirteenth century
weaponry. This terminology goes smoothly and evocatively with
Vance's great skill at concocting ringing place-names and other
kinds of proper names, particularly because these all tend to be
derived as if from local British usage; for instance, three places
in "The Dragon Masters" are called the High Jambles, Banbeck
Jambles, and the Slicten Slides, although all three are just different sizes of talus-slopes—and Vance uses that term for them,
just once and with apparent reluctance.

It then follows naturally that Vance's dragon-haunted, beautifully named landscapes are very small, and the wars that rage
across them take place in a geographical compass more easily
imaginable as a part of northern Scotland than as the surface of
a whole planet. The map supplied by *Galaxy's* artist at the opening of "The Dragon Masters" shows that at least one other reader
shares this feeling with me; the whole territory looks as constricted as one of the more rural and stony parts of Vermont,
and the text of the story gives exactly this impression of the
terrain. Despite the chanting of many other place-names which
may stand for other parts of Aerlith—a whole planet—the action
of the novel takes place in two valleys and in the rough country
which surrounds and divides them. Had it happened in Westport,
nobody in Scarsdale would have heard a thing.

I have no objection to this; it fits perfectly the kind of world in
which Vance works by preference, and he works in it with beautiful consistency. But it is a fantasy world, and one with a small
compass: limited in geography, limited in social customs, limited
in range of invention except for the less constricted flourishes
of its magic.

106

Magic, for Vance, has often meant telepathy, but he seems to be more at home with physical magic—magic that affects the real world, without the requirement that people read each other's minds before anything can happen. Vance's characters, unlike Schmitz', start out by failing to understand each other, and go on from there to even more grievous misunderstandings until nothing will serve but that one of them kill the other; which is what happens in "The Dragon Masters." This is the oldest form of magic, a weapon of aggression, best used by the most acute intelligence against the less acute; the reading of minds is a recent and soggier notion, but suitable as a weapon between medieval men, and a mark of weakness in an alien enemy (Vance makes both points in this story). For Vance, the world of magic is a world of dragons, and here he has invented a marvelous lot of them—one set of which is human, or at least started out that way; it is a world of battles, hand-to-hand wherever possible; and a world of physical magic, some of which partakes of the ritual notions of science fiction (in particular, the genetic magic of Stapledon). And above all it is a world of heroes, struggling against tremendous odds within a very small frame, and uninterested in any thoughts but their own.

Don't miss it; but don't expect it to be science fiction, in the sense that the Thomas is science fiction.* The two stories are as remote from one another as Raymond F. Jones and E. R. Eddison.

---

*At the 21st World Science Fiction Convention in Washington, D.C. (1963), where the Vance won a Hugo as the best science fiction novel of 1962, editor Fred Pohl quoted me as ruling that the story wasn't science fiction, but said that in his opinion it was, because "genetics is a science." I think he must have missed my qualifier, as well as the parenthetical reference to Stapledon immediately above it. Surely the novel is science fiction, of a sort—but its sort is not the sort of "hard" science fiction, firmly based in technology, that is written by such authors as Jones, Thomas, Anderson, Clement, and others down to and including me; its affinities are closer to fantasy, which in the hands of a master has other rewards.

THOUGH IT HAS GIVEN ME BACK MY
job, it nevertheless saddens me to see that every generation of
writers seems fated to learn even the simplest matters the hard
way. I'm not referring to dubs, either—with due obeisance to
Damon Knight's point that it's a waste of spirit to deploy heavy
artillery against black-beetles—but to new writers in whom I
have, or am trying to have, an emotional investment.

My example is Dean McLaughlin, who is almost alone among
the latest generation in being a writer of "hard" science fiction.
(In the preceding generation there are three—Budrys, Dickson,
and Garrett—but of these, Budrys is a law unto himself, and
Garrett has spent much of his career in what seems to me to be
a deliberate campaign to throw away all his virtues except his
industry.) McLaughlin is still a rather imitative writer, as
could only be expected for such a late starter, but all the in-
gredients of a major science fiction author have been there from
the beginning: a good ear, a respect for the language, a solid
background in technology, a reverence for facts, and a fine,
free-wheeling ingenuity.

In the August, 1962 issue of *F&SF* he seems determined to
bury all of these gifts in cliches. "The Voyage Which Is Ended"
might serve as an anthology of all the beginners' mistakes that
have been committed since Cain edited Abel. I have talked about
all these bloopers before, but what is even more important is
the fact that they are none of them prejudices of mine. Every
professional writer should have been aware of them long before

WILLIAM ATHELING, JR.

I was born, and it's depressing to see them still being perpetuated by a writer of McLaughlin's firm gifts and high promise.

Let us take, to begin with, said-bookism. This is defined as the systematic avoidance of the verb "said," in a misguided search for variety. I once slashed away at a truly flat-headed, square-eared, three-footed first story (Zirul's "Final Exam") for this kind of silliness, but to see McLaughlin doing it alarms me more.

"The Voyage Which Is Ended" is a 12-page story in which, essentially, only one thing happens, and that has already happened in the title; the rest of the copy presents characters talking and otherwise reacting over it. Of the 85 speech-verbs used in the story, 36 are "said," and the rest are, with very few exceptions, clumsy and unnecessary attempts to avoid "said." Of the avoidances, the largest number tell the reader something that he can already see in the content of the speech: tell (4), remind, ask (4), demand (2), explain (2), agree, repeat (3), invite, object (2), protest ("inarticulately," which must have taken some doing), claim, echo (2), urge, argue, admit (4), reply, state, protest, wonder, and persist. My favorites in this group are the three repeats of "repeat" and the two echoes of "echo," but you are invited to select your own.

Of possibly *necessary* alternate speech-tags, which describe how the speaker sounded when he spoke, there are only a few: grumble, hiss, exclaim, breathe, murmur. They are all commonplace and difficult to defend in context, but at least the proportion is about right; your ordinary said-book addict uses so many of these that he makes his characters sound like a hi-fi demonstration record. The remaining tags cannot be defended at all, since they are the usual verbs having nothing whatsoever to do with speech: beam, smile, shrug, frown. ("Good morning," he polevaulted.*)

I repeat, this is not an exclusive Atheling prejudice, though I was complaining about it in *Writer's Digest* a good fifteen years ago. Five years before that, unbeknownst to me, Wolcott Gibbs was telling *New Yorker* writers:

> Word "said" is O.K. Efforts to avoid repetition by inserting "grunted," "snorted," etc., are waste motion and offend the pure in heart.

---

*A friend of mine tells me she knows a man who can do this.

110

Similarly, Gibbs noted that

> ...writers always use too many adverbs. On one page
> I found 11 modifying the verb "said." "He said morosely,
> violently, eloquently, so on." Editorial theory should
> probably be that a writer who can't make his context
> indicate the way his character is talking ought to be in
> another line of work. Anyway, it is impossible for a
> character to go through all these emotional states one
> after the other. Lon Chaney might be able to do it, but
> he is dead.*

Dean is, thus far at least, not a very determined grunter or
snorter, but his adverbs are certainly on the verge of running
away with him. In addition to the character who protests inarticulately, he has one who echoes grandly, and among his
minority who simply say things may be found people who say
them tersely, efficiently, gravely, stiffly, quietly, mildly, carelessly and hollowly.

I protext, Atheling swallowed tautologically.

Second: It has always seemed to me that since Flaubert it is
inexcusable for a writer to flip back and forth between one
character's point of view and another's unless he has some
limited, special reason for it, over which he is totally in control.
I wouldn't insist upon this rule in the novel, where there may be
a larger number of reasons for shifting viewpoints, and in any
case there is room to establish a number of different viewpoints
without confusing the reader as to who is now looking at and reacting to the events. But in the short story, a unified point of
view is by now virtually mandatory; I would grant an exception
only to the rare and difficult story which depends upon the
cumulative effect of a mosaic of events.

"The Voyage Which Is Ended" is not a mosaic story, but it
flops around among viewpoints like a landed eel. On the second
page, it drops for two paragraphs out of the viewpoint of Capt.
Griscomb—the only defensible viewpoint character—into the
mind of his secretary, and her viewpoint keeps popping into his
throughout, even inside single paragraphs ("She caught herself
and chuckled awkwardly"—students of said-bookism may take
time out to admire the second formulation, too). Every so often,

*First printed in James Thurber's The Years With Ross, Simon & Schuster, 1957.

the omniscient author drops like Thackeray down from Heaven ("If there was anything left to say, neither knew what it was"). Then the viewpoint goes back to Griscomb, and then again momentarily is looking at the scene through the eyes of a minor character ("He stopped when he realized Griscomb wasn't going to laugh").

There is a lot more that might be said about this story, mostly in sorrow: Its high budget of sentences with no verbs in them; its exacerbating, soap-opera way of beginning interior monologues with the word "Yes"; its standard adolescent moodiness over an outworn situation; its loose, floppy construction; its pseudo-cosmic, organically meaningless attempt at a punchline.... Shall I go on? No. I can only pray that Dean will give up trying to imitate the Martha Foley story and get back to writing hard science fiction. If he gives that up for this kind of damp cat-crap, we will have lost the only writer of his generation of whom we could have expected genuinely solid work. A writer as good as McLaughlin is an idiot to waste a minute of his time repeating other people's mistakes, or imitating other people's idioms.

In this issue, too, editor Avram Davidson bravely classifies five of his stories as fantasy, five as science-fantasy (a term specially revived by his predecessor /independently of H. G. Wells, who meant something else by it/ to cover the Aldiss "Hothouse" series), and five as science fiction. This matter of definition is a real can of worms, as Avram knows as well as anybody. I have mentioned before my adherance to Sturgeon's Definition, which however doesn't purport to cover anything but a *good* science fiction story. Questions of quality aside, it seems to me that anything one wishes to call a science fiction story should contain some vestige of some knowledge of some science.

By this minimal criterion there is only one science fiction story in the issue, this being Rosel George Brown's, which exhibits a more than considerable knowledge of microbiology. The story itself is as smooth as immersion oil and very funny; Mrs. Brown is just about the only one of *F&SF's* former gaggle of housewives who doesn't strike me as verging on the feeble-minded; in fact, I think her work has attracted less attention than it deserves.

The issue also contains a piece by Randall Garrett which might, by a conscious effort, be called marginal science fiction, if one allows that psychology might some day become a science. All the same, I can see no reason why the same story couldn't have happened aboard a submarine, a criticism to which many hundreds of stories about spaceships are subject. Finally, we have the cover story by Fritz Leiber, which presents a complex case indeed.

Let me say at the outset that I think "The Secret Songs" is a lovely story, and that the remarks that follow only indicate the ways in which I think it could have been better still. Essentially, it explores the fantasies and hallucinations of two mental hospital outpatients who are maintaining themselves on drugs: He on tranquilizers (including beer), she on benzedrine. The effects of these drugs are well known, and part of Leiber's contribution is simply to show what kinds of personalities use them as crutches, and what in our society fosters such illnesses. The combination is both ferocious and sad.

Sounds like a mainstream story, doesn't it? But I have left out the crucial point. The story is not science fiction, but it's *about* science fiction...the male character reads the stuff and his hallucinations are derived from it (mostly, apparently, from Lensman stories). In other words, what we have here is another in the long series of science fiction essays in incest. The medium is already specialized and cultish enough to put off most outsiders, because of the commonly accepted practice of borrowing magical terms ("overdrive," "subspace") without explaining them; but when it begins to feed on itself, it takes another long step into the incomprehensible for all but its most experienced readers.

There was no need for this. True, the public atmosphere these days is pervaded with material for science-fictional hallucinations, from flying saucers to real sputniks, and it is as logical for a character to go bats in this direction as in any other. But this assumption—which I once made the mistake of making myself—immediately classifies as science fiction a story which otherwise might have won itself a much wider audience.

I cannot speak for Fritz, but I know that in my own case the essential reason for creating so unnecessary a mixture was timidity. I had a mainstream novel going—a *Bildungsroman* with a backdrop of contemporary science, called *The Frozen Year* (Ballantine, 1957)—and I should have stuck to it. Making my madman's delusions science-fictional was a last-minute retreat

113

into the genre with which I was most familiar, and in which I could be moderately sure of a sale. Well, I sold it; and there it sits, a piece of spoiled goods. On the basis of this experience, I suggest that the temptation to write *about* science fiction in a story may well mean that the story is not science fiction at all, and shouldn't be handled as such.

AT THE WESTERCON THIS YEAR, I took an opportunity to ask Anthony Boucher why British newspaper reviews of science fiction were so superior to the American. Tony's answer was that British reviewers in most fields are better than American.

This is quite true, but it isn't really an answer; it's just a more generalized version of my question, which continued to nag at me. Since then I've drawn some conclusions of my own. To document them, let me describe the situation itself first.

I subscribe to clipping services in both the United States and Great Britain. My experience with American reviewers confirms what most readers have suspected: (1) They are mostly lousy, and (2) They are about to become extinct.

To take these points in order, those reviewers who still pay any attention to science fiction in the general press consist primarily of morons. My definition of a moron under this rubric is a reviewer who reprints the jacket blurb of a book, verbatim. If he then signs his own name to this copy, he is also a villain. However, I prefer to reserve the epithet "villain" to the snow-job reviewers who say that they like science fiction, but who, when confronted with a single specimen that they actually do like, go out of their way to tell their readers that this isn't *actually* science fiction at all, but something far superior. We have one of that breed in New York, whose face and generalized praise of science fiction once appeared regularly on the back cover of *F&SF*. I think that if that magazine's publisher had any

115

inkling of the amount of active damage Orville Prescott has done the field, he would have expunged Mr. Prescott's portrait and his hypocritical endorsement long ere this.

Mind you, I don't object to Mr. Prescott's praising an occasional science fiction novel, and I certainly don't ask that he praise them all. I object solely to the fact that he obviously wants both to ride the band-wagon, if there is one, and at the same time to follow it at a safe distance, in case it should break down.

Last—and I'm sorry I have to place them last, but I do—we have the remaining experts, like Tony himself, and P. Schuyler Miller. I have paired these names with care. Tony occasionally gets his valuable opinions into such places as the New York *Herald Tribune*. These days he is just about the only expert who does. Schuy Miller is one of the few remaining reviewers in our own orbit who is worth reading, and he too represents a vanishing breed. Compare the Golden Age of book reviewing in the magazines; then we had a choice of Tony himself, Schuy, Damon Knight, Frederik Pohl, Lester del Rey, Ted Sturgeon, Henry Bott (sorry—I got carried away for a second). Where are they now? Personally still with us, thank goodness, but their professional criticism is by-and-large no longer available, and I must say that I miss it.

And all of the good ones that remain—I count two, or perhaps three—have fallen victim to the notion that a reviewer of science fiction ought also to review popularizations of science. I have fulminated about this before, so I'll confine my remarks on it here to a brief summary. I personally am only slightly interested in the opinions of any science fiction reviewer, even Schuy, even Fred Pohl, on a popular science book. I can get better opinions from real experts on the subjects these books deal with. I respect Fred and Schuy and a few other people I know as dedicated amateurs in certain scientific fields; but if I really want to know the value of a given book in such a field, I will go to a dedicated professional, like Loren Eiseley, Ernest Nagel, or Isaac Asimov. What I want to hear from Fred, or Schuy, is what they think of a piece of science *fiction,* where they are not just dedicated amateurs, but reigning experts.

As for my second point, that even in the United States these people are becoming extinct, I need only point out to you how few professional science fiction magazines today carry any book review column at all. The clippings that I receive from other

THE ISSUE AT HAND

American sources, that is, newspapers and the like, have been
declining steadily in the last ten years, and now have reached
the point of near-invisibility. Most other science fiction writers
I know who are clipping collectors—and who among us is not—
could tell you very much the same story. My American clipping
service, which is supposed to cut for me nothing but book reviews,
has become so nervous about earning its money and keeping my
custom that it recently sent me a Xerox duplicate of the first
installment of the *Playboy* panel (July/August, 1963), and I had to
notify them, I'm afraid a little stiffly, that they were not supposed
to clip what I wrote, but only what was written about me.

In San Francisco I also asked Tony why it was that science
fiction reviewing in this country had declined so sharply, and
his answer was that the quality of published science fiction in
the last ten years had taken such a turn for the worse that it was
no longer considered worth the space to review it. With all due
respect, I must reject this explanation, for two reasons. First
of all, it seems to me that it is not a reviewer's function to review nothing but good books. Tony would certainly reject that
approach for his New York *Herald Tribune* column about detective novels, for instance. After all, if a book is a thoroughly
bad example of its type, the reader deserves to be warned of this,
just as much as he deserves to be touted on to a good example.
Furthermore, this reason of Tony's runs squarely against the
English experience, which is the next thing I would like to expose
for you.

During the same period that the American reviews that I was
receiving were declining so markedly, the number of English
reviews was rising. I don't know the exact present ratio, but I'd
guess that it's about twelve to one. Yet British writers produce
as much bad science fiction as we do. Indeed, I would say that
where their best is pretty consistently better than our best, their
worst is far below the level of the worst products that are coming out in the United States now. When John Wyndham is good,
he is very, very good, but when Charles Eric Maine is bad, he is
horrid. (I should add here that I have never seen a Maine book
that was less than bad.)

Yet British reviewers seem to feel as obligated to review these
awful novels of Maine's as they do the superior books of Wyndham
and Clarke, and I quite agree that that is part of their function.
To make this contrast even more pointed, I should like to offer

an incomplete list of the British periodicals from which I have quite recently received clippings. In fact, these clippings are so recent that I haven't yet had time to paste them up in my scrapbook. The list goes like this:

The *Times* of London, the *Times Literary Supplement,* the Manchester *Guardian,* the Oxford *Mail,* the Glasgow *Herald,* the *Illustrated London News,* the Nottingham *Guardian-Journal, Punch,* the *Tablet,* and a scattering of reviews from smaller publications, a small proportion of which, alas, are reprints of the jacket copy. If you are at all familiar with the press of the British Isles, you will have noted that these are the major periodicals of England, and in fact the names include those of two of the greatest newspapers in the world. This is in pretty sharp contrast to the New York *Times,* which last reviewed a science fiction novel just a little after the Bronze Age, and to the *Herald Tribune,* which has a slightly better record, but only slightly.

In addition, most of these British reviews are thoughtful, thorough, and by knowledgeable writers. At present, for example, the chief science fiction reviewer of the London *Times Literary Supplement* is Kingsley Amis. The chief science fiction reviewer for the Oxford *Mail* is Brian Aldiss. And even where a British review is by someone whose name I don't recognize, I can usually count upon it to be as informed and unfrivolous as most of the work of these two distinguished gentlemen. Amis, Edmund Crispin and Robert Conquest were at last reports the three people who made up the Board of the British Science Fiction Book Club—that is to say, the three people who are involved in actually selecting the books the club members will get. In contrast, I do not know who it is who selects the titles for Doubleday's Science Fiction Book Club over here, but I have long suspected that it is the same team of two snapping turtles and an aardvark that used to write the ads for that organization. And I say these harsh words in despite of the fact—or perhaps some of you would say because of it—that one of my books was happened upon by this trio.

These facts, I think, provide a clue to the whole situation; and I've recently had some confirmation of my theory which I would like to pass along to you. My most recent submission to my British publishers—Faber & Faber, may they live forever—was an exceedingly difficult manuscript, and something quite different from what they were accustomed to receive from me. As a result, they called in outside help. Because the manuscript was a historical novel, one of the two outside readers they engaged was an eminent British historical novelist who is a specialist in the period that I was writing about. And because, perhaps, they wondered if I had snuck some science fiction into the thirteenth century, they called in a reader who knew my past writing, and therefore might have some gauge of what the historical novel was like compared to my past level of performance.

They then sent me both of these readers' reports. Never in my entire publishing history have I ever seen anything even remotely like those reports. They were analyses in depth, done with knowledge and care, in detail and at considerable length. I'm not at liberty to tell you, I'm sorry to say, who the historical novelist is, but the science fiction expert Faber & Faber called in was Brian Aldiss.

Both reports were enormously valuable to me, and to the novel; and thereafter, Faber assigned as my particular editor on this project an absolutely searing fireball named Ann Corlett who in effect sat down across the ocean with me and went through the book practically line by line to get it into what we both agreed ought to have been its shape in the first place. No editor I have ever worked with over here, with one shining exception, has shown so much initial understanding of what it was that I had set out to do, plus so enormous a technical grasp of why I hadn't succeeded in doing it.

I think the conclusions one must draw from all this are inescapable. English reviewers and reviews, English publishers and English editors, are so much better with science fiction, and probably with other categories of fiction as well, than their American counterparts, because they actively care about what it is that they are doing, and the other people they assign to work with the author or on the work also actively care about it, and what is perhaps even more important, know something about it. That situation, by and large, simply does not prevail at the present time in the United States.

Now, what can be done about this? I have an answer of sorts —and I think some of you will recognize it as a small campaign I have been carrying on now for several years. I've discussed it in the pages of fan magazines, I commented on it at the Westercon, and I'd like very much to expose it again here.

Who in the United States does know something about science fiction? Who in the United States does care something about it?

WILLIAM ATHELING, JR.

The answer to that is very simple.

You do.

If writers in this country cannot for the most part get responsible, informed and loving criticism—and criticism can be none the less loving for being harsh—from editors, or from book reviewers, it has to come from you. And the only way it can come from you effectively is through a general revival of the letter columns in the professional science fiction magazines.

There is hope for such a revival. Just in the past year, two magazines, *If* and *F&SF*, have started letter columns. Thus far, they are pretty tentative. They must not be allowed to remain so. You and I have had a long time to get out of the habit of expressing our opinions to the magazines, and I've no doubt that we're all quite rusty at it. But if the editors become convinced that we actively want these columns, they will survive, and other magazines will bring them back.

It is, I am well aware, a very small start on this rather large problem. But after all, we have to start somewhere.

A Question of Content *September, 1960*

I HAVE BEEN WONDERING WHAT IT IS about science fiction that so attracts its readers and writers. What are we seeking when we turn to stories about other times and other worlds? Why do most of us prefer a story set in the future to every other kind of story, even though almost all such stories are both unredeemably bad and very remote from any experience we are ever likely to encounter? What does it do for us, that we cling to it in this strange way, though to an outside observer it doesn't seem to merit a tithe this much devotion?

Well, there is that odiously familiar word "escape" lurking in the wings, but even if we assume it to be valid, it is too broad to be useful, for the obvious reason that it fails to explain why many people who want to escape choose this particular, narrow little branch of fiction instead of some other. All of the easy answers I've encountered thus far have similar defects, and this includes a couple of psychoanalytic hypotheses that would curl Philip José Farmer's hair.

But the stubborn fact remains. When I say that we cling to science fiction, I am talking even more about writers than about readers, or even fans. A good many scornful things have been said about science fiction readers, but all the evidence shows that they are better read outside their hobby than are most other devotees of specialized fiction—those who love detective stories, say, or Westerns. Most of those people seem to read nothing else at all (including one recent, if somewhat absentee President). Even the science fiction writer, when you look at him as a reader,

WILLIAM ATHELING, JR.

is often very catholic in his tastes. I know a few, and I don't
think they're at all freakish, who strike me as being quite erudite
outside their specialty; the first one who occurs to me here (but
there are a large number of them) is Avram Davidson, who seems
to know everything about everything.

But except to turn a mechanical buck, most of them will write
nothing but science fiction, no matter what else they like to read.
This is perfectly true of me; I have been reading the stuff for
thirty years, and writing it for twenty, until now it bores me
almost to the point of insanity, and yet I can't leave it alone, and
I really don't want to. At the 1959 Milford Science Fiction
Writers' Conference, the group was polled one evening on how
many present were then involved in some writing project outside
science fiction. Every single hand was raised, and at the 1960
Conference there was an identical unanimity. This would seem
to undercut my point rather drastically, were it not for the fact
that I simply don't believe in that show of hands. At least, I
have yet to see a serious non-science fiction work from any of
these people.

I don't doubt that some of them raised their hands because
they were also engaged in counterfeiting ribald classics in broken
English for the men's magazines, or ghosting an autobiography
for some paper napkin tycoon, or feeding copy to a sports car
journal; that's the kind of buck-turning that every professional
writer finds on his hands from time to time—and it's amazing
how much better they pay than science fiction does—and maybe
they can be regarded in the same light as the copy that Clifford
D. Simak turns out for the excellent newspaper he works for
(the Minneapolis *Star*), or the copy that I do for my advertising
agency. And of course serious work takes time; I've been waiting more than a year to see some of this output, but that may
not be long enough.

But I think many of those hands were raised only because the
boys and girls were worried about the state of the market, and
because they felt that they *should* be developing a few sidelines.
I don't believe that they were. In fact, if you ask yourself how
many writers science fiction has had in its whole history who
wrote other kinds of fiction as competently, or even tried to, you
will not be forced to take off your shoes to reach a total. Most
of us, after writing a detective story, or a popular medical
article, or a speech for a company president, return to science

122

fiction with relief, with the feeling that this is what we really like
to do, no matter how small the checks are.

Why should this be? Any sane writer would work in this field
only now and then, for kicks, because he has an idea that he just
can't resist. But that's not how much of us behave. We go on
and on, year after year, churning out science fiction—about five
hundred of us, if you please, in a field that can't print the total
output of more than fifty, and maybe not as much as twenty-five.
We do it not because each piece is irresistible, and might also
turn out to be good, but because we love the stuff, even when it's
dull and we're sorry we undertook it to begin with.

As for the readers—and I have enough enemies already, so I
don't mind a few more—I don't know how else one can account
for the grand passions that have been raised by Edgar Rice Burroughs, H. P. Lovecraft, A. Merritt, and a number of technically
still living people whom the law of libel forbids me to mention,
except by the conclusion that boredom in our field is not necessarily the enemy of love.

This subject was touched upon by the Guest of Honor, Poul
Anderson, at the Detention (the 17th World Science Fiction Convention, 1959), and had he made it his central subject I should
find myself with no problem on my hands. But Poul's own subject
was an appeal for a unitary approach to science fiction, in which
philosophy, love, technology, poetry, and the elements of daily
life would all play important and roughly equal roles. Now, this
is an ideal prescription for science fiction, and it is nowhere
better exemplified than in Poul's own novel, "The Man Who
Counts" (*Astounding*, February/April, 1958. Reprinted in paperback contemptuously retitled—by Ace—*War of the Wing-Men*,
1958). But it is a good prescription for science fiction only because it is a good prescription for fiction as a whole. No good
fiction of any kind has ever been produced in any other way, and
I feel safe in saying that none ever will be.

One-sided novels may be satire, or allegory, or "key" novels
—the kind of novel where you don't know what's going on until
you discover that the character named Horace Mills FitzCampbell
is really Henry Luce—but they are never complete novels, with
rare exceptions, and they have about as much lasting power as a
piece of Kleenex. This description fits most science fiction very
well, and Poul did a thorough job of expanding upon the point.
But it seems to me that Poul's unitary principle also goes a long

way toward explaining why popular or critical successes like George Orwell's *1984* (Harcourt, Brace, 1949), Kurt Vonnegut's *Player Piano* (Scribner's, 1952), Bernard Wolfe's *Limbo* (Random House, 1952), Aldous Huxley's *Brave New World* (Doubleday, 1932), Franz Werfel's *Star of the Unborn* (Viking, 1946), and so on, never increase our audience or the prestige of our idiom. We have asked ourselves time and time again why this should be. I think I have the answer, but I am not sure.

Many of these books turn on gimmicks which to us are old and stale, and usually they handle those gimmicks clumsily and with varying degrees of naivete. Yet they command an audience and a respect which our much more experienced practitioners, like Asimov or Anderson or Simak, can't even get close to. Nor does this happen because the books were written by Big Names. This *was* true of Franz Werfel's last novel, but it was his least popular work. Huxley was only moderately well known when he wrote *Brave New World,* and a science fiction novel written after he was world-famous, *Ape and Essence,* was a flat bust. Orwell had no reputation as a novelist—he had written only one, *Keep the Aspidistra Flying,* which was dreadful, and everybody said it was dreadful; Wolfe and Vonnegut were virtually unknown; and you may remember that Herman Wouk's attempt to muscle into our field, undertaken when he was the fair-haired boy of *Time* magazine, got no farther than *Collier's* ("The Lomokome Papers," February, 1956) before dying of sheer unworthiness to live.

Nevertheless these successes can be accounted for. Each of these "outside" authors can easily be seen to be *thinking* about something. George Orwell was not simply pushing about the counters of that old science fiction plot about the future Asiatic-type despotism in hopes of finding an angle fresh enough to sell. He had something fundamental to say about one of the great philosophical problems of all time: The nature of the relationship between the individual and the state. It is small wonder that people, particularly in our time, snatched up that book as though it were bread in a famine. It's of no importance that Orwell's futuristic devices look a little seedy to this jaded audience. What is important is that the proposition he set out to show us is perhaps the most important contribution to this problem by an artist since Sophocles wrote the *Antigone,* and perhaps the first original such contribution since then. This proposition—the drive-wheel of *1984*—is only six words long: *The purpose of*

THE ISSUE AT HAND

power is power. Not wealth, not luxury, not fame, not a woman a day, and most certainly not the public welfare, but the naked enjoyment of power for its own sake. To most of the kinds of people who are attracted to politics, power is not a means to another end, but is in itself the greatest possible of all ends. This is a blood-curdling notion, precisely because so much of history seems to support it—particularly recent history—but not only does it shock, it commands attention, in a way that the rats and the torture-machines in the very same chapter can't possibly do.

The central subject of Kurt Vonnegut's *Player Piano* is the Second Industrial Revolution, the cybernetic revolution, already well under way, which is likely to terminate with the great bulk of mankind, including most of its educated citizens, with nothing to do or to sell which will be worth anybody's money to buy. This is a good science fiction subject, and there's certainly nothing essentially new about it. The marvels of a machine civilization, in which human beings are freed from toil, is one of the oldest science fiction themes. But Vonnegut raised the question, *Leisure for what?* Most people have no more capacity for leisure than they have for creative mathematics or corporate management. Just how Utopian can a civilization be in which most people sit around staring blankly at each other, waiting for the next ball game or the next bowling match or until it's time to eat the next meal? And just how long will they sit still for it? The prospect is immediate, Vonnegut makes it seem immediate, and the reader knew that he was personally involved, not just being amused.

Werfel asks very much the same sort of question. In his case it read, *Personal immortality for what?* In *Star of the Unborn,* you will recall, people didn't die—they were scientifically changed into a sort of vegetable organism and planted, so that in effect they lived forever (presuming, I suppose, that somebody else watered them). But the process sometimes went awry, and produced monstrosities. Since these were irreversible, they were just thrown away. The monstrosities had a tendency, too, to resemble whatever character defects a man had in his original life. A grasping man, for instance, might turn into a huge, flopping hand and arm; a lecherous man—well, you can see the possibilities. Here again, personal immortality in the flesh is an old science-fictional subject, which I have written about my-

125

WILLIAM ATHELING, JR.

self, but the question of what is to be done with all those years
seldom comes up. When it is raised, there is usually a little
ritual about how wonderful it would be to have all those lifetimes
to become expert in some subject, or to pursue some gigantic
project, or to perfect some craft—outcomes which just might be
possible for one out of a thousand of us. For the rest of us, the
chances are much better that we would simply wither, like
Tithonus, or vegetate mindlessly, like Werfel's flowers, or to
become more and more single-mindedly and monstrously the
same kind of cripple or sinner that we were during our first
seventy years. For Werfel, who was a Roman Catholic, it was
perfectly obvious that the human psyche isn't built to take immortality of the flesh; to me, an agnostic, his conclusion seems
one hundred per cent right.

So here we have Orwell talking about the problem of power;
Vonnegut about the problem of goals; Werfel about the problem
of time and mortality. Bernard Wolfe, in *Limbo,* was interested
in two big facets of the problem of evil: the question of why men
fight, and why they suffer. Here, I think he didn't come within
miles of supplying a convincing answer, in fact he simply took
over a little Freudian voodoo from the late Dr. Edmund Bergler,
but nevertheless his subject was one of the big ones—the kind of
subject that stirs readers whether they like science fiction or
not, and whether or not they agree with the author's approach to it.

In short, all these books are about something. I submit to you
that very few science fiction stories, even the best of them, are
about anything, and that in this sense they fail Poul Anderson's
unitary test in the worst possible way. For all their ingenuities
of detail and their smoothness as exercises, they show no signs
of thinking—and by that I mean thinking about problems that mean
something to everyone, not just about whether or not a match
will stay lit in free fall, which is a gimmick and nothing else.
In that realm they are about as interesting as rope-dancing,
trick roller-skating, or any other act on the Ed Sullivan television
show, and like most such acts they are fatally preoccupied with
imitating each other.

And what happens when a general reader, fascinated by Werfel
or Vonnegut or Orwell, steps into our field for more of the same,
perhaps at the invitation of *Life* magazine? He may very well
notice that what he is now reading is more adroit in some ways,
but probably he won't, and anyway that one gain isn't going to

last him long. General readers and critics may be taken in temporarily by small ingenuities which are new to them, but only temporarily. That is not the kind of thing they admire in fiction, nor should they. Nor are they seeking to have their sense of wonder stimulated. The genuine sense of wonder, a piece of standard equipment in the human brain, can get along very well on what is commonplace to the distractible. It does not need to be bludgeoned by an endless succession of concocted and visibly spurious marvels. Anti-matter, galactic collisions, and numbers with long strings of zeroes after them do have their fascinations, but none of them is nearly as awe-inspiring as a five-year-old girl who happens to be yours.

Now I know that *Science Fiction Times* isn't going to award me any headlines for having come out four-square in favor of father-hood. All the same, it is true that "Wonders are many, but none so wonderful as man." Yet you may read several hundred science fiction stories a year without finding more than one which reflects any consciousness of this banal and ancient axiom. The writer or reader who still thinks an exploding star is inherently more wonderful than the mind and heart of the man who wonders at it is going to run out of these peripheral wonders sooner or later, and then perhaps he will blame the readers or the writers or the editors or the benighted public—we have seen this process going on for a long time. What he is now seeking from fiction of all kinds, science fiction included, is not the sense of wonder, but the sense of *conviction*. That is the feeling that the story you are reading is about something that is worth your adult attention, and that the author approached it in that light.

Some few works of science fiction are as serious and as rewarding as anything their authors might have attempted outside our field. Arthur C. Clarke's *Childhood's End* (Houghton Mifflin, 1953) and Theodore Sturgeon's *More Than Human* (Farrar, Straus, 1953) both pass my proposed test magnificently, and I am sure you will have other candidates for such a list. I also happily grant any writer full marks for trying, even where I am not sure of the artistic success of the effort; for this reason I am delighted that both Robert Heinlein's *Starship Troopers* (Putnam's, 1960) and Kurt Vonnegut's *The Sirens of Titan* (Dell, 1959) won Hugo nominations, and distressed that George O. Smith's *The Fourth R* (Ballantine, 1959) did not—the Smith has its lacks, but it is about a subject of consequence, honestly approached. But I have the awful feeling that many of us continue to read science fiction and to write it for no better reason than that it is comfortable and safe. No matter how outlandish it looks to outsiders, we grew up with it, and we're used to it.

I think it manifestly impossible to write well about any subject which you regard as comfortable and safe, or to read it well if comfort and safety is all you're seeking. Good science fiction is neither. It is precisely the science fiction story that rattles people's teeth and shakes their convictions that finds its way into the mainstream—and by this I don't mean ikon-smashing, as ably exemplified by Pohl's and Kornbluth's *The Space Merchants* (Ballantine, 1953). Once an ikon is smashed, you're out of business until you find another one; Madison Avenue is certainly a tempting target, but it won't last forever. The great problems will. I feel certain that people will still be reading Theodore Sturgeon on the variety and nature of the love relationship long after the advertising boys have wrought their final offense and gone home, no longer available for satirization. This is the reason people will still read *The Brothers Karamazov* but won't even open *Uncle Tom's Cabin*. Chattel slavery is dead, but the problems discussed in *Karamazov* are still with us, and they always will be.

I am trying to discuss the kind of book from which the reader emerges with the feeling, "I never thought about it that way before"; the kind of book with which the author has not only parted the reader from his cash and an hour of his time, but also has in some small fraction enlarged his thinking and thereby changed his life. For this kind of operation an exploding star is not a proper tool; at best, it is only a backdrop.

Isn't that, in fact, what we all felt about science fiction when we first encountered it? It's still a young field, and most of us encountered it as youngsters. It was a wonderful feeling, that sense that interplanetary space was not only there to be looked at, it was there to be traveled in—which the scientists themselves were busily denying that we would ever be able to do. We felt bigger thereby, because what we were reading made our world seem bigger. But both we and the field are not children any longer, and we have reached the stage where our physical horizons can't be extended much more without bursting the bubble of the physical universe itself. The ethical, the moral, the philosophical horizons remain, and those are infinite. It is there, I believe, that the realm of good science fiction must lie.

Before his death, my dear friend Cyril Kornbluth had come to roughly the same conclusion; I quote from his essay in *The Science Fiction Novel* (Advent: Publishers, 1959; 1964):

> We are suspending reality, you and I. By the signs of the rocket-ship and the ray gun and the time machine we indicate that the relationship between us has nothing to do with the real world. By writing the stuff, and by reading it, we abdicate from action; we give free play to our unconscious drives and symbols. We write and read, not about the real world, but about ourselves and the things within ourselves.

This is true, but it is not all of the truth. The real world is not different from what we have inside our skulls; in fact, all we know about the real world is what we have inside our skulls. This dichotomy that Cyril described is not a real dichotomy. The real insides are what make fiction, and if it is not about that it is just gadgetry and talk. This is where good fiction has always made its land and home, and I think that now either we must invade it, or else become just another brackish little backwater of literature, as deservedly forgotten as the mannerisms of Euphues.

Is there something that can be done about this? Well, the only place in our field where any kind of influence can be exerted upon what gets written—not upon what gets bought, mind you, but what gets written—is in the voting for the Hugo awards. I have no personal reason to complain about the Hugo nominations, since I was given one, but it has often happened in the past—not only in science fiction, but in other fields—that popularity contests are not won by the best man. Though Poul's appeal for unitary science fiction in 1959 was a most eloquent one, it did not seem to reach many of the voters who made 1960's nominations. I would like to try it again.

Next year, when the magic time comes around and you have made up your list of five or ten possibles in each category—and particularly in the novel, because this is where trends are made and influences most noted—I suggest that you put aside your other reasons for admiring your choices, just temporarily, and ask yourself about each title that you have put down: *Is it about anything?* Nothing could be better for the health of our field than to let every science fiction writer know, beginning right now, that from now on there will be no escape from this question.

Index

"AAA Ace" Series, 91
Abel, 109
Abernathy, Robert, 93
Abramson, Ben, Publisher, 49
Ace Books, Inc., 123
Adam, 57
Advent: Publishers, 22, 44f, 129
Aldiss, Brian W., 112, 118, 119
AMAZING STORIES, 18, 23, 44
AMERICAN SCIENTIST, 98
Amis, Kingsley, 118
"An Answer of Sorts," 97
ANALOG SCIENCE FACT - SCIENCE
  FICTION, 101, 104, 105
"And a Star to Steer Her By," 80
Anderson, Poul, 71, 72, 73, 74, 105, 106,
  107f, 123, 124, 126, 129
Anderson, Sherwood, 21
Antigone, 124
"Anything You Can Do!," 105
Ape and Essence, 124
"Armistice," 90
Arnold, Matthew, 73
Arrowsmith, 33
Asimov, Isaac, 29, 30, 43, 74, 75, 93,
  116, 124
ASTOUNDING SCIENCE FICTION, 17, 19,
  29, 30, 39, 42f, 43, 44, 45, 50, 55, 67,
  71, 78, 79, 80, 82, 86, 87, 89, 123
Atheling, William (pseudonym of Ezra
  Pound), 8-9
Atheling, William, Jr. (pseudonym of
  James Blish), 7, 8, 9, 20f, 34, 38f, 40f,
  42f, 52, 58, 59, 60, 72f, 78f, 82, 103,
  110, 111

Audel's Handy Wiring Manual, 46f
Avalon Books (Thomas Bouregy & Co.),
  40, 59, 61
Axe, 7

"Baldy" Series, 76, 78
Ballantine Books, Inc., 57, 58, 59, 93f,
  113, 127, 128
Barchester Towers, 63
"Beatrice," 24
Believers' World, 59
Benedict, Steve, 36
Benson, Hugh, 53, 54
Beowulf, 16
Bergeron, Richard, 7
Bergler, Edmund, 126
Bester, Alfred, 19f, 41, 98
"Big Planet," 16, 41
Blish, James, 7-9, 22, 48, 51, 52, 53,
  55, 56, 74, 75, 76, 107f, 113, 114, 122
"Bobbsey Twins," 75
Boggs, Redd, 7, 9, 11f, 21, 35
Bott, Henry, 116
Boucher, Anthony (pseudonym of William
  Anthony Parker White; see also other
  pseudonym, H. H. Holmes), 23, 25, 26,
  27, 29, 30, 36, 54, 55, 71, 72, 73, 74,
  75, 93, 115, 116, 117
Bouregy & Curl (see also Avalon), 27
Brackett, Leigh (Mrs. Edmond Hamilton),
  74, 75
Bradbury, Ray, 14, 15, 17, 23, 28, 46,
  53, 54, 55, 74, 75, 76, 77, 78
Brave New World, 20f, 124
British Broadcasting Company, 58

131

INDEX

Foley, Martha, 112
"Fool's Errand," 53
"Fool's Mate," 36
"For I Am a Jealous People," 58
"Foundation" Series, 30, 99
"Four in One," 39
Fourth R, The, 127
France, Anatole, 15
Frazer, James George, 49
Freud, Sigmund, 67
Fritch, Charles E., 14, 15, 17f, 81
Frozen Year, The, 113
FUTURE SCIENCE FICTION, 47, 48, 76

GALAXY SCIENCE FICTION, 13, 18, 38, 42, 45, 55, 89, 90, 91, 98, 105, 106
Galileo (Galileo Galilei), 57
Gallun, Raymond Z., 44
Garrett, Randall (see also Darrel T. Langart), 31, 74, 75, 76, 104f, 109, 112
Gault, William Campbell, 36
"Gavagan's Bar" Series, 94
Gentile, Carl, 73
Gernsback, Hugo, 44
Gibbs, Wolcott, 110, 111
Gilbert, William Schwenck, 75
"Girl in the Ice, The," 93
Glinka, Mikhail Ivanovich, 38
Gold, Horace L., 13, 18, 19, 23, 27, 30, 36, 55, 92
Golden Apples of the Sun, The, 76
"Goodly Creatures, The," 28-29
"Gravy Planet" (see also The Space Merchants), 20
Gresham's Law, 59
Grolier Encyclopedia, 34
Guardian, Manchester, 118
Guardian-Journal, Nottingham, 118
"Gulf," 67

Hamilton, Edmond, 46, 74
Harcourt, Brace & Co., 124
Hardin-Simmons University, 58
Harness, Charles L., 22, 27, 28
Harris, Larry M., 31f
Healy, Raymond J., 54
Heinlein, Robert A., 30, 42, 50, 62, 63, 64, 65, 66, 67, 68, 69, 70, 79, 127
Hemingway, Ernest, 73f
Henry, O. (pseudonym of William Sidney Porter), 38
Herald, Glasgow, 118

Herald Tribune, New York, 97, 116, 117, 118
Hillman Publications, 16
Holmes, H. H. (pseudonym of William Anthony Parker White, see also other pseudonym, Anthony Boucher), 36
Holst, Gustave, 68f
Holt (Henry), & Co., 54
Homer, 39, 73f
"Homo Saps," 31
"Hothouse" Series, 112
Houghton Mifflin & Co., 127
Hubbard, L. Ron, 22, 74, 75
Huggins, Roy, 23
"Hugo" Awards (see also Hugo Gernsback), 57, 63f, 107f, 127, 129
Humphreys, Emyr, 93
"Humpty Dumpty," 78, 79
"Hunting Lodge, The," 31f
Huxley, Aldous, 20f, 124
Hyman, Stanley Edgar, 23

"I Am Nothing," 42f
IF SCIENCE FICTION, 51, 55, 120
Illustrated London News, 118
"I'm Looking for 'Jeff'," 24
"Immortal Game, The," 71, 73
"In Hiding," 71
In Search of Wonder, 22
"I've Got a Little List," 74, 75

Jackson, Shirley, 93
Janifer, Laurence M., 47
Jones, Raymond F., 30, 31, 107
Journal of the British Interplanetary Society, The, 57
"Joy Ride," 36
Joyce, James, 72f, 78, 102
Judd, Cyril (pseudonym of Cyril M. Kornbluth and Judith Merril), 48
Jung, Carl Gustav, 56f

Keep the Aspidistra Flying, 124
Kidd, Virginia, 53
Kinsmen of the Dragon, 22
Knight, Damon, 9, 17, 21, 22, 30, 33, 34, 39, 52, 76, 78, 81, 89, 97, 109, 116
Knight, Norman L., 30
"Know Thy Neighbor," 36
Kornbluth, Cyril M. (see also Cecil Corwin), 20f, 28, 29, 36f, 47, 48, 90, 91, 128, 129
Kubilius, Walter, 48

INDEX

INDEX

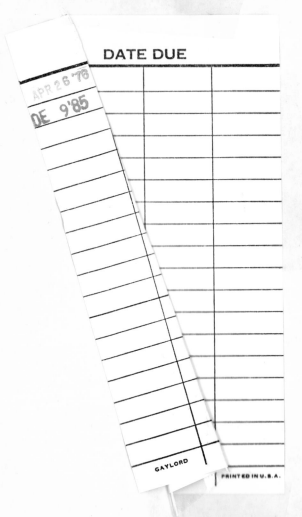

DATE DUE

GAYLORD   PRINTED IN U.S.A.